Las Cruces

Pictorial Researcher Tim Blevins

Manuscript Reviewer Linda G. Blazer

Proofreader Darlene A. Reeves

Las Cruces

An Illustrated History

Linda G. Harris

Published by
Arroyo Press
P.O. Box 4333, Las Cruces, New Mexico 88003
(505) 522-2348

Printed in the United States of America
99 98 97 95 94 93 5 4 3 2 1

Library of Congress Cataloging-in-Publication Data

Harris, Linda G.
Las Cruces--an illustrated history / by Linda G. Harris. -- 1st ed.
Includes bibliographical references and index.
ISBN 0-9623682-5-3
1. Las Cruces (N.M.)--History--Juvenile literature. 2. Las Cruces (N.M.)--Pictorial works--Juvenile literature. [1. Las Cruces (N.M.)--History.] I. Title.
F804.L27H36 1993
978.9'66--dc20 93-22913
CIP
AC

On the Endsheets: *Artist Joseph Ireland captures the legacy of the Mesilla Valley in this painting of the Rio Grande and Doña Ana Mountains. Ireland is a nationally published artist whose affection for the Southwest prompted his relocation from Seattle to the Mesilla Valley in 1987.*

For Jim, my boon companion

TABLE OF CONTENTS

FOREWORD

Unique is a word to be used with caution, but by definition it can characterize the city of Las Cruces as "not likely to be duplicated."

When the majestic spires of the Organ Mountains were forged in the awesome furnace of creation and thrust up through the silent encompassing seas, time measured by thousands of years began the evolution of earth and water that made life possible here for its early people. Life was harsh for them, sheltering in mountain caves; neither was it easy for the ones who ventured down to the valley and the river. But the land blessed by the sun inspired a fierce loyalty among those who survived danger from the elements and fought for possession and use of the land and water to make the valley their home.

Only the vital and the vigorous survived the ardors of those days to become the founders of Las Cruces. Undeterred by the crosses that marked the graves of massacred travelers, they chose to name the town for the crosses as symbols of hope, not death. The town drew to itself newcomers diverse in background but alike in the optimism and foresight who recognized and grasped opportunity. The rich natural resources of fertile land and managed water combined with pioneer energy to make the desert bloom.

The town has grown into a city. Las Cruces has been able uniquely--there's that word again--to retain the values of the past while reaching toward growth and change. The crossroads of time and place bring together the heritage of the past and the promise of the future.

The present links together what has gone before and what is yet to come in a symbolic relationship. The fires of creation that fuel the thermal fields near the city hold great promise of industrial expansion. The primeval energy that lifted mountain and mesa united altitude and weather to give it one of the world's best climates. That in turn made Las Cruces the birthplace of the rocket research that led to America's space effort. Surely the area is the logical port for launching to the stars.

This history of Las Cruces maps the crossroads of time and the elements, and by analysis in depth demonstrates how the desert blooms.

And not less importantly, why "our mountains" are so beautifully unique.

LEE PRIESTLEY

PREFACE

Once when I was covering an agricultural tour for the university, our busload of observers passed near a spot where in 1896 a judge and his son had disappeared, supposedly murdered. As talk of the mystery buzzed among us, a retired professor stood and took a place at the front of the bus. His cowboy father had been one of the men tried for and acquitted of the crime. The professor wanted us to know his side of the story. As I listened, it struck me that the history of this valley could still be told in the words of its sons and daughters. Now, more than a decade later, I have had the opportunity to string together the stories of these remarkable people and of the events that have shaped life in this valley. It has been a pleasure.

I never could have written this book without the librarians, archivists and their staffs at New Mexico State University and at Branigan Memorial Library who took on my enthusiasm for the project, guiding me through their collections and recommending sources.

I have great affection for New Mexico State University and am indebted to those who searched files, sent snippets of information, and made their research and expertise available. I am also indebted to those outside the university who unselfishly gave me access to their own unpublished research.

For unraveling the mysteries of various sciences I thank the experts who took the time to help me. And for providing me endless information I thank the unsung and unseen public information officers in agencies and offices throughout the county.

Without fail, I found people generous and enthusiastic with their expertise and advice; many have become friends. Finally, I gratefully acknowledge my late friend Della Kilcrease whose unfulfilled wish was to write the history of this valley.

The Land by the River

Prehistory - 1692

The mountains could be distinctly traced in the moonlight, and but for their serried peaks to remind us now that we were upon terra firma, it would have required no great stretch of the imagination to believe ourselves at sea.

CAPT. W.W.H. DAVIS, *El Gringo*

The mountains preside over this valley like smug chameleons, changing their color and their character almost at will. Their high slopes, brushed with green under a brilliant August sky, just as easily can take on the reflected glow of a winter's fiery sunset. And on some misty mornings, when clouds spill over their cold, gray peaks, they remind us they dwell among the heavens. Like the long-ago Greeks who worshiped their Olympus, those of us who live in this valley look upon the Organ Mountains with possessive reverence. They are *our* mountains. And they are the most beautiful in New Mexico.

But back in the murky recess of geologic time, some 570 million years ago, the land was dominated by a vast shallow sea whose floor was layered with sand, mud and limestone, the construction material for mountains to come. The sea's last retreat 138 million years ago signaled the end of the age when dinosaurs paddled along the shore, leaving footprints at the water's edge. In their place came camels, bison, the wolf and the coyote to roam the changing New Mexico landscape.

Beginning about 40 million years ago volcanoes in central and southwestern New Mexico erupted in a fury that would continue for the next 20 million years. These enormous explosions, like the silent seas before them, were mountain builders. Collapsing in a convulsion of ash and magma, these volcanic craters hardened over millions of years as they became covered by cooling layers of sediment. The origins of the Organ Mountains

The Organ Mountains *(previous pages) have long been a favorite subject for artists and photographers. Pamela Porter captured the timeless solitude of the mountains in this modern-day photograph.*

Distinctive and rugged, *the Organ Mountains are part of the Rocky Mountain chain 10 miles east of Las Cruces. Juan de Oñate referred to them as Sierra del Olvido, the "Mountain Range of Oblivion." In the 1680s Gov. Antonio de Otermín called these mountains Los Organos, or "Pipe Organ," after the peaks that resemble the pipes of an organ.*

began as such a volcano some 32 million years ago.

About that time, the earth's stretching and twisting also was causing the crust to thin and crack, creating a pair of subterranean fault zones that formed the boundaries of an ever-widening wedge running from central Colorado down through the middle of New Mexico and into Texas. The Mesilla Valley and the Jornada del Muerto straddle the wide southern end of this wedge, known as the Rio Grande Rift. Over the next 15 million years the Organ Mountains gradually were raised along the eastern edge of the rift, where wind and water stripped away their sediment coating to reveal jagged granite spires. Along the rift's western edge giant volcanoes vented their energy, scattering ash hundreds of miles and then exhausted, collapsing to form gaping craters.

Undermined by the faults, the rift slowly began to give way causing great blocks of the crust to sink, in some places as much as five miles. These sunken blocks created a series of basins extending hundreds of miles along the rift's length. Over millions of years, wind, water and gravity joined forces to fill the basins with the rocky debris shorn from neighboring mountains. In turn, the gravely basins became reservoirs catching runoff from nearby mountain streams. At first the elongated basins were isolated from each other, but as the climate became increasingly wetter, the pools began to overflow into adjacent basins. Eventually, the waters high in the Colorado Rockies threaded their way from basin to basin until they reached the Gulf of Mexico in one unbroken flow. Thus was the Rio Grande born some 600,000 years ago.

Ancient hunters and foragers first appeared in the Mesilla Valley about 10,000 years ago, lured south by the abundance of game inhabiting the bordering mountains and the river marshes. Here, hunters tracked ground sloths, mammoths and buffalo to the Rio Grande where the prehistoric giants became bogged in the river's muck, defenseless against the hunter's spear. Hunting parties also had their choice of smaller game such as deer, antelope,

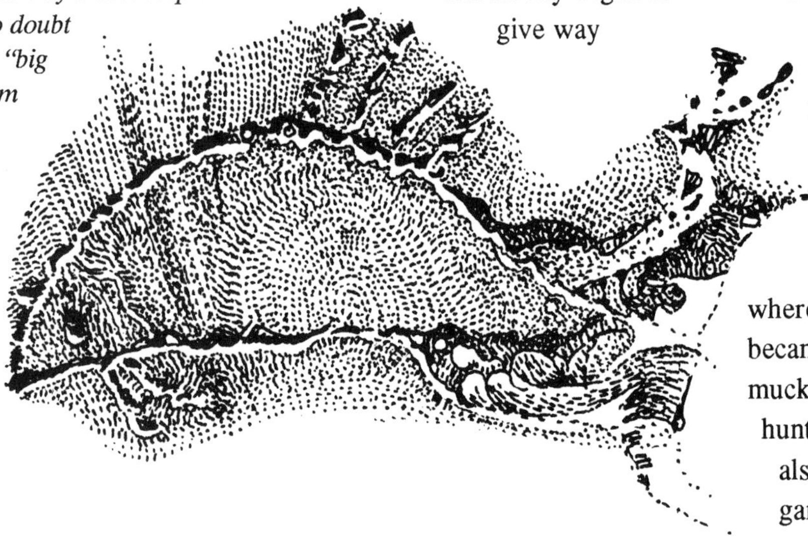

Petroglyphs *pecked into rocks in Doña Ana County's Lucero Canyon provide clues to the lives of ancient inhabitants. This fish petroglyph recreated here by artist Joseph Ireland no doubt refers to a "big catch" from the Rio Grande.*

and at least a dozen species of camel. These ancient nomads traveled in small family bands stopping at *parajes,* or encampments, for a few days or weeks before moving on in their round of hunting and gathering.

Starting about 7,000 years ago, an increasingly arid climate began to transform the valley's lush grasslands into a landscape predominated by mesquite, creosote and yucca. The domain of prehistoric giants, now extinct, became the undisputed territory of smaller game, down to the scrawniest desert rat. As the surrounding desert became less hospitable, the ancient nomads turned increasingly to the river's green corridor for their sustenance.

By the time of Christ, these hunters and gatherers reluctantly had given up their wanderings for the structured village life of the farmer. The people of the Mogollon culture, as they are now identified, learned to make soups and baskets from the yucca plant, and flour from mesquite beans. And they expressed their cultural beliefs through circles, zig zags, and pictures of snakes and stick "dancing" figures pecked into the rocks.

Just north of the Mesilla Dam where the riverbank rises to the west was once a Mogollon village called Las Tules, named by archaeologists for the cattails growing nearby. Farmers lived here about 900 A.D. in pit houses near their fields where they grew drought-resistant maize and close to the river where they fished for turtles. The dozen or so Las Tules homes, small rooms actually, were dug partway into the ground, with their thatched roofs visible above circular or rectangular foundations. These early home builders found pit digging easier than the laborious process required of adobe-like construction. They saved their scarce wood supply for roof supports, and used their abundance of sand for flooring. The walls in some pithouses were plastered, while others were left bare, depending evidently on the industry of their owners. Even burials were carried out efficiently, taking as little effort and space as possible. Corpses were neatly packaged, arms folded, knees drawn to chest, and crammed into tight little graves.

But more than their houses, it was their pottery that revealed the austerity and isolation of village life. Las Tules potters fashioned round bottomed jars from brown river clay, leaving them unglazed and unpainted, without so much as a handle.

Over the next 200 years in settlements like Las Tules, the villagers traded their pithouses for *jacales.* These aboveground huts were built with walls of upright poles lashed together and plastered with mud and roofed with brush and small limbs. Some lived in small rectangular homes built of coarse adobe. Instead of abandoning their pithouses, however, villagers used them for storage and as ceremonial rooms, the forerunner of the kiva. During this time, the villagers began to trade with those from other Mogollon settlements, bartering their brown ware for the black on red pottery of the Three Rivers people who lived in the Sierra Blanca Mountains.

By 1300, an extended drought had led the farmers to build irrigation ditches from the river to their fields where they grew corn, squash and beans to feed an exploding population. For safety, convenience and sociability, the growing communities grouped their flat-roofed adobe homes around a plaza or lived in long two-story apartment-like structures. Inside these pueblos they cooked and kept warm over basin shaped fire pits. They likely used their large communal rooms for feasting and celebrations, adorning themselves for the occasion with macaw feathers and copper bells imported from Casas Grandes in Chihuahua, and turquoise and jet from the Sacramento Mountains. In trade they offered their own pottery, now also patterned in red and black.

Sometime around 1450 life along the Rio Grande proved too fragile and the people began leaving, or dying. Pueblo villages up and down the valley became deserted, maybe because of drought, or invading Apaches. But no one really knows why.

The wane of civilization in the Mesilla Valley, and indeed the entire Southwest, coincided with the age of discovery and exploration in Europe. The union of science and technology in the 15th and 16th centuries was to open the seas to lands undreamed of and allow the Europeans to colonize fully half the world by 1900. Of these adventurers, none were more courageous, more daring or more enduring than the Spanish conquistadors. These extraordinary people, full of restless energy, held strict

An ancient bowl *from the Three Rivers area north of Tularosa is characteristic to the natives there who painted their terra cotta pottery with fine geometric designs, drawn in red.*

loyalties to their king and their religion, along with a consuming ambition for wealth and social status. When Hernando Cortés and his 500 men conquered the Aztec empire with such ease in 1519, it confirmed the bold Spaniard's belief in his New World destiny. Unfortunately for the Aztec ruler Moctezuma, his gifts to the invaders (including gold, emeralds and pearls, along with amazing feather headdresses decorated with gems, and "books" written in hieroglyphics) revealed the riches the Spaniards had hoped for.

The first Spaniard to visit the Mesilla Valley was an accidental tourist by the name of Alvar Nuñez Cabeza de Vaca, who in November 1535 came walking into a village just above present day El Paso. Cabeza de Vaca and his three companions, half-starved and half-naked, were the only survivors of an expedition shipwrecked off the Texas coast in 1528. The fortunate four (their compadres either drowned or were eaten by cannibals) were enslaved on Galveston Island. After a year Cabeza de Vaca escaped and fled into the Texas interior where he became a trader and a medicine man of sorts. Some five, lonely years later he met up with the other three survivors and with the help of native escorts, the ragged band

Alvar Nuñez Cabeza de Vaca *and the few survivors of a 1528 shipwreck, made their way back to Mexico after years of wandering the Texas plains and passing through what is today Southern New Mexico. After arriving in Mexico City, Cabeza de Vaca told the authorities of the Seven Cities of Gold, although he never actually saw evidence of them.*

found its way out of the wilderness. In Mexico City, the refugees arrived just in time for the Fiesta de Santiago and a "bullfight and tournament." Warmly received by Viceroy Antonio de Mendoza and Cortés, the accommodating Cabeza de Vaca, in the wishful thinking typical of the Spanish conquistador, reported seeing "many fine signs of gold, antimony, iron, copper and other metals . . ." during his seven-year odyssey in the wilderness.

At the time, Viceroy Mendoza had in his service the bright, ambitious son of a lesser Spanish noble who had come to Mexico seeking his fortune. Undoubtedly, the handsome Francisco Vásquez de Coronado quickly saw his opportunity in Cabeza de Vaca's optimistic tale. The young Coronado, in the viceroy's favor and able to finance the trip, was the government's choice to lead the first expedition into the Southwest. In 1540, Coronado set out in search of the Seven Cities of Gold. He took with him 336 men (including several priests), the wives and children of a few of the soldiers, several hundred Indians, and 559 horses. He was all of 30 years old. Although he never set foot in southern New Mexico and his expedition ended in disappointment, Coronado had opened the way for the adventurous of another generation.

For forty years after Coronado's wayfaring, no Spaniard ventured into the lands along the Rio Grande. Discouraged by Coronado's failure, the bearded men diverted their energies to a spectacular deposit of silver discovered at Zacatecas, northwest of Mexico City, in 1546. The strike brought a stampede of miners and prospectors to the frontier, creating mining barons overnight.

Then one crisp January morning in 1583, Spaniards once again appeared at the Rio Grande. Antonio de Espejo, along with 15 soldiers, two friars and their Indian servants had stopped to refresh their horses at a watering hole at the southern edge of the Mesilla Valley near present day Canutillo. They were in search of three brave but foolish friars who had embarked on a missionary expedition into New Mexico two years earlier. After learning the friars had been murdered, Espejo, like any enterprising Spaniard, then set off on a 3,500-mile journey throughout the region looking for gold.

As was the custom, Spanish expeditions included an observer whose duty it was to chronicle the deeds and the discoveries of the venture. These accounts, written in descriptive, often lyrical prose, tell of life along the Rio Grande from the not always objective Spanish viewpoint.

From the account at Espejo's camp at Canutillo, came word of a new people occupying the

The jacal, *a house built of wood poles plastered with mud, evolved little since the Las Tules villagers began fabricating their homes with mud and brush. A few structures like this turn-of-the-century jacal still can be found in the Mesilla Valley.*

region. The Manso, as they would later be called, inhabited the river pass where there were "numerous reeds and large marshes and pools with quantities of fish close by the river." During the expedition's week-long stay at the pass, the Mansos brought them mesquite and corn, and fish caught in the pools with small dragnets. Although these small robust Indians led the temperate life of fishermen and farmers, they could be as fierce as the Mescalero Apaches inhabiting the mountains to the north. The Spaniards found the Mansos who lived at the pass, as well as those living in the Mesilla Valley, similar to natives they had seen to the south. As did the southern Indians, the Manso men went naked, except here, the chronicle notes, "the men tied their privy parts with a small ribbon," probably as a charm against evil spirits. The Manso male devoted great attention to his hair, which was cut bowl-shaped to just above his ears. He sopped his cap of hair with blood or paint to stiffen the corkscrew curls radiating from his crown. For accent, he left one long lock to which he fastened feathers from geese, cranes and sparrow hawks. The women, dressed in deerskin vests and skirts, wore their hair unadorned, tied simply on top of their heads.

These hospitable people greeted Juan de Oñate's arrival in 1598 with the cry *"mansos y amigos."* Their declaration as "gentle and friendly" people no doubt was as much a precaution

CANTO I

I sing of arms and the heroic man,
The being, courage, care, and high emprise
Of him whose unconquered patience,
Though cast upon a sea of cares,
In spite of envy slanderous,
Is raising to new heights the feats,
The deeds, of those brave Spaniards who,
In the far India of the West,
Discovering in the world that which was hid,
'Plus Ultra' go bravely saying
By force of valor and strong arms,
In war and suffering as experienced
As celebrated now by pen unskilled.

Gaspar Pérez de Villagrá

against attack as it was a sign of friendship. In any event, Oñate, the colonizer of New Mexico, who would also become its first governor, acknowledged the overture by christening them with the name Manso.

Juan de Oñate was born on the rough frontier of New Spain. His father, Cristóbal de Oñate, had accumulated vast landholdings during his service under Coronado. And like many Spaniards, he took a serious interest in prospecting. In the barren foothills some 400 miles northwest of Mexico City, Zacatecos Indians had shown Cristóbol and his partners outcroppings streaked with silver. These mines at Zacatecas eventually would yield one-fifth the world's silver. There in 1552 Juan de Oñate was born in the town his father had founded near the mines that one day would finance the colonization of New Mexico.

The young Oñate was shaped as much by the hard edge of the frontier as he was by his father's wealth. As a teenager he had fought in Indian wars against the ferocious Aztec tribe of Chichimecas. For 20 years Oñate fought the Indians and as head of his own expedition, claimed vast new lands under the Spanish banner.

Oñate was New Spain's ideal aristocrat. He was wealthy and brave, and he was married to a descendant of both Cortés and Moctezuma. But he was 46 and looking beyond his father's realm toward New Mexico. His goal was to colonize New Mexico and perhaps repeat the fabulous silver discovery at Zacatecas. But by the time he set out for New Mexico in February 1598 he had endured three long years of bureaucratic delays, and spent his fortune on the venture.

In early April, Oñate's advance party of eight horesemen finally reached the Rio Grande just below El Paso after four days without water. "Our men, consumed by the burning thirst, their tongues swollen and their throats parched, threw themselves into the water and drank as though the entire river did not carry enough water to quench their terrible thirst," wrote Gaspar Pérez de Villagrá, Oñate's loyal and poetic historian. The huge caravan of 400 people, 83 wagons and 7,000 head of stock soon joined the soldiers on the shady banks of the river. Quickly, they prepared for the official ceremonies in which Oñate would claim New Mexico as Spain's newest acquisition.

On the morning of April 30, 1598, all was ready. In a makeshift chapel under the cottonwoods, Franciscan priests celebrated a solemn high mass and Fray Alonso Martínez preached an "excellent sermon." Then, as befitting a Spanish festival, some of the soldiers performed a play about the adventures of the friars in New Mexico, written for the occasion by Capt. Marcos Farfán. In high spirits, the people then gathered for the formal proclamation. Horsemen wearing their most "gala attire . . . and glistening armor" drew up in formation, while the rest of the colony lined the way for the governor. Through the crowd, Oñate came forward, proud and distinguished, wearing one of his six suits of armor. He was flanked on one side by the crucifix and on the other by the Spanish standard. At the river's edge he took the flag and with his own hands planted it in the soil, taking possession of New Mexico in the name of the holy Trinity and "of the most Christian king, Don Philip." With that, trumpets were sounded, guns were fired and a "great demonstration was held."

The Mansos certainly could not have missed the commotion caused by the wandering tribe of Spaniards. A few days later, they helped Oñate's men find a place to ford the river above El Paso. The soldiers persuaded four of the Indians to accompany them back to camp where the governor had them clothed and loaded them with gifts. "The natives were delighted," writes Villagrá, "and soon returned with a great number of their friends bringing us great quantities of fish." (Half a continent away, the colonists at Plymouth would share in a thanksgiving feast similar to the one on the Rio Grande 22 years earlier.)

Bartolomé de Las Casas, *the most celebrated priest in the Americas, spoke against the harsh treatment of the natives by their Spanish masters. In particular Las Casas condemned the encomienda system, whereby the governor could "give" certain Indians to colonists to use as they might choose. The encomienda, Las Casas said, was "a moral pestilence . . . invented by Satan." Largely through his efforts, Spain instituted the New Laws, which called for an end to slavery, the easing of labor requirements, and reforms of the encomienda system.*

A short distance up river, the colonists passed what would later become the site for Las Cruces. Just beyond on May 21 the colonists buried sixty-year-old Pedro Robledo, the first of the colonists to die in New Mexico. The great bluff overlooking his burial ground became known first as the Paraje de Robledo, and today as the Robledo Mountains.

This wild and abandoned region was but a prelude to what they later found to be true of all New Mexico. Spain's newest colony was not a land of silver and gold, but the inhospitable homeland of destitute natives. Although their intent was to settle this harsh land and Christianize the Indians, they soon lost the desire for either. Up north, events took a tragic turn. When a small party of Oñate's men stopped at Acoma Pueblo to obtain food, the Indians lured them near the cliffs where they were attacked. Thirteen men, including Oñate's nephew Juan de Zaldívar and one of Pedro Robledo's sons, were killed.

When word of the ambush reached Oñate, the anguished governor assembled the survivors at his headquarters for a formal hearing. Based on the testimony from the his soldiers and backed by the legal opinion of the friars Oñate made the decision to attack and crush Acoma. The assault lasted three days, killing 600 to 800 Indians and burning the pueblo to the ground. The survivors suffered nearly as cruel a fate. All males over 25 had one foot cut off and were sentenced to 20 years of slavery. Women and younger males also were forced into 20 years of servitude.

At the end of his decade as governor, Oñate was a failed man, burdened by his trials as governor, and defeated in his attempts to find silver. In 1614 he was tried for crimes of colonial mismanagement (including the massacre at Acoma), for which he was fined and condemned to perpetual exile from New Mexico.

After his disasterous term as governor, Oñate concentrated his energies on rebuilding his neglected Zacatecas mines. Within a decade the mines had replenished the Oñate fortune. In 1623 King Philip IV finally reimbursed Oñate his fine. Although his banishment from New Mexico still stood, Oñate felt vindicated. The next year the king named him to the prestigious post of mining inspector for all of Spain. While on an inspection tour in June 1626, Oñate, the son of a silver baron, collapsed and died in a silver mine. He was 74.

Though his leadership seemed a failure, his cause was not. Through Oñate, Spain had made its indelible mark on New Mexico. During his tenure, a supply service was organized to provide goods for New Mexico's missions, but in practice actually handled all the commerce in New Mexico during the 17th century. Oñate's earlier route became the Camino Real, or the Royal (official) Road, where caravans departed from Mexico City traveled through the Mesilla Valley and into Santa Fe. On the trip north the wagons carried mission supplies and on the return trip they hauled staples of hides, piñon nuts and blankets. Later, sheep would be exported

The late morning sun *on the Organ Mountains reveals deep crevices and narrow fissures along its granite slopes. For centuries travelers along the Camino Real have been awed by the impassable appearance of the Organ peaks, some of which reach an elevation of almost 9,000 feet.*

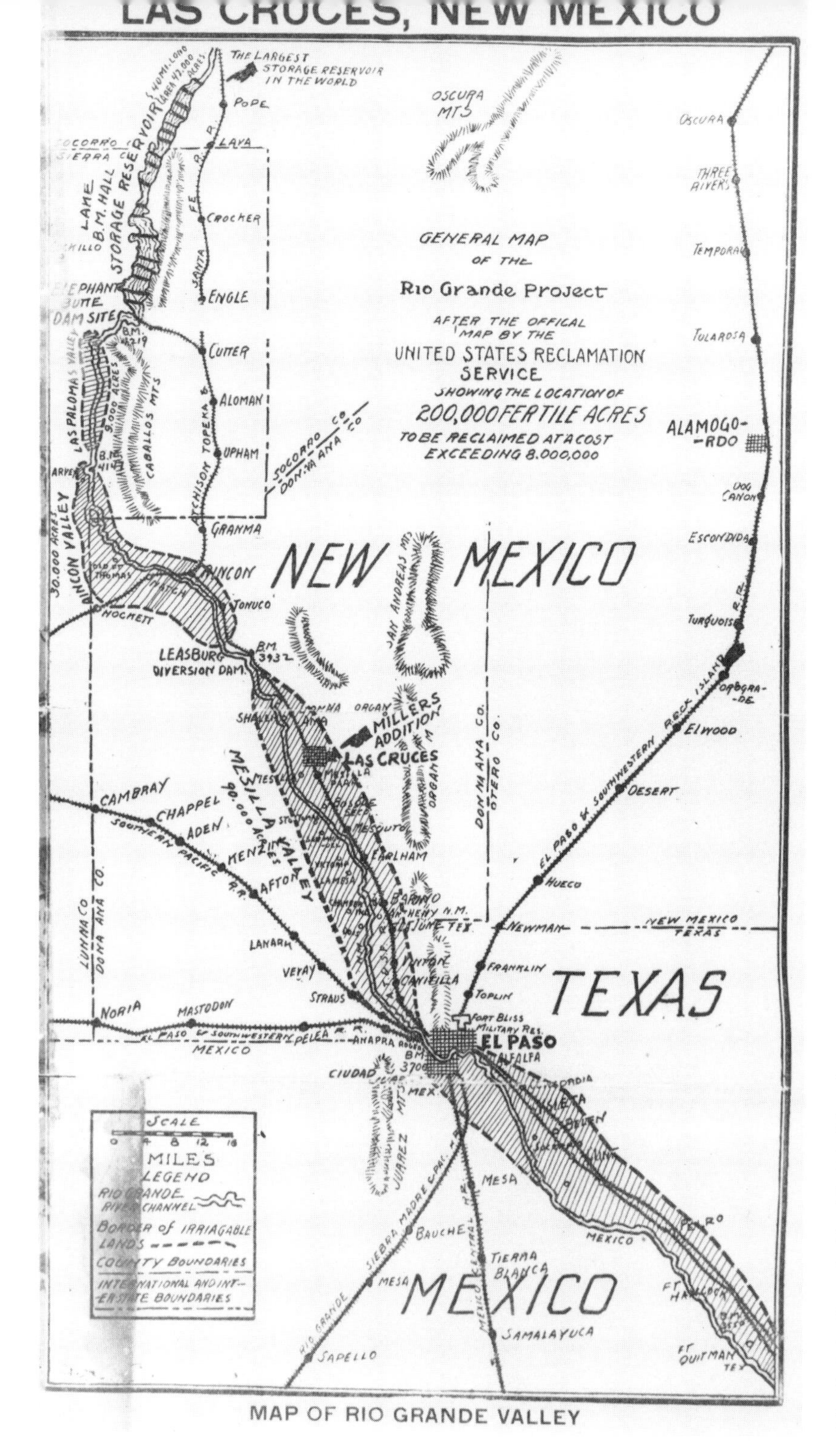

Las Cruces was the most important city in Southern New Mexico by 1909 when this U.S. Reclamation Service map was drawn. Unlike the isolated territory of earlier times, the valley had become extensively irrigated, and was well-connected by railroad to major cities in four directions.

along with Indian slaves for the mines. The fact that the church controlled the only supply route underscored its importance in the remote colony.

The priests believed God had chosen them to convert the heathen of the New World and the soldiers were more than willing to help. The historical impression of the friar in his linen robe and sandals walking alongside the Spanish soldier astride his fine horse is a true one. The priest was in search of souls, the conquistador, wealth. But in pursuit of their dual mission, they treated the Indians shamefully.

By the late 1670s, New Mexico was in a sad state. The non-Pueblo population numbered about 3,500, but a large proportion of them were mestizos, of mixed blood, who held weak loyalty to the government. Nearly half the population, Indian and non-Indian alike was starving. The missionaries, determined to stamp out the Indian religion had prohibited native ceremonies and destroyed their kivas. Indian leaders were whipped and imprisoned. One such leader was Pópe, who on Aug. 10, 1680, led the Pueblo Revolt in which one-third of the white population in New Mexico was killed.

On the first day of the revolt, Governor Antonio de Otermín, in near panic, gathered his people and their livestock into the compound at Santa Fe. One unconfirmed report had all the settlers below Santa Fe massacred, while another rumor said the revolt had spread to El Paso where the supply train destined for Santa Fe had been destroyed. After a nine-day siege, Otermín and his people were allowed to make their retreat for El Paso. Along the way, they picked up survivors and learned that Father Francisco Ayeta and his caravan were waiting in El Paso. Through the miserable August and into September, the refugees, mostly women and children walking barefoot, made their way down Oñate's road to a camp near Canutillo. There they were met by Father Ayeta's pack train.

In October the 2,000 hungry refugees were moved to El Paso, sorted into groups and assigned, along with accompanying priests, to three settlements in the valley. The friars, were adamant about keeping the refugees separate from the natives to protect the Indians from Spanish "diseases and vices." Also, it would be easier to keep an eye on these smaller groups to prevent them from deserting Otermín's command. Descendants from these refugee settlements would one day colonize the Mesilla Valley.

In the meantime, El Paso served as the temporary capital of New Mexico, and Otermín set about the depressing chore of reporting the disaster to the viceroy. Otermín was faced not only with the task of holding together his ragtag group, but of mustering troops to reconquer Santa Fe. Plagued by desertions, and "burdened by so many women and children," he could count only 155 fighting men. In November 1680 he led this small contingency to retake New Mexico but at Santa Fe was driven back to El Paso. It is no wonder the beleaguered governor, suffering from severe headaches, pleaded in a letter to Father Ayeta, "For the love of God and Saint Anthony as soon as you arrive in Mexico, do everything you possibly can to get me out of here." Not until 1691 would Otermín be relieved of his responsibilities.

The new governor, with a flourish reminiscent of Oñate, in 1692 led 200 soldiers and a group of priests into the ruined capital of Santa Fe. Announced by trumpets and drums, Don Diego de Vargas proclaimed that he had not come to punish the Indians but to pardon and convert them. During the next 12 hours he returned time and again to repeat his offer to the amazement of the Indian sentries on the rooftops. The daring, but diplomatic governor then entered the courtyard of the Palace of the Governors, unfurled the Spanish banner, and proclaimed New Mexico once more a part of the Spanish empire.

Courage and Crosses

1700 - 1848

Once among the pastoral valleys and the desert bench terraces that yield silt, the river is ever after the color of the earth that it drags so heavily in its shallow flow.

PAUL HORGAN, *Great River*

During the 16th century Spain had built a great empire and uncovered the riches of the new world. But it was a nation of adventurers, not shopkeepers and so by the 1700s Spain had let its fortunes slip into the hands of English, Dutch and French merchants. While its colonies on the American continent were struggling to survive, England's flourished and grew to a population of 300,000 energetic souls pushing against the western frontier.

New Mexico, as the viceroys saw it, was the last barrier against the ambitions of the English and French and they fought to isolate their province from these foreigners. Key to their defense was the economic protection of trade between Mexico City and Santa Fe. The merchants of Chihuahua, who had gained control of the former mission caravans, dominated commerce in 18th century New Mexico.

Their trade route from Mexico City followed Oñate's original wagon trace through the Chihuahuan Desert to the Rio Grande and north to Santa Fe. Their annual caravans along the Camino Real, the royal road, brought high-priced finished goods (fine fabrics at $25 a yard) to be traded for sheep (at $1 a head), and other plentiful raw materials at Taos and Santa Fe. Fear that outside trade would break their profitable monopoly, the Spanish government had forbidden their subjects along the Rio Grande to trade with foreigners.

Year after year, merchants and missionaries followed Oñate's wagon trail through the

The largest river *in New Mexico (previous pages) has been known by many names, including Rio Grande, Rio de las Palmas, and Rio Bravo. Here the river passes beneath the Robledo Mountains near the old Shalam Colony site.*

***Apache hunters** may have hunted mule deer in the Organ Mountains with their bows during the early 1800s. Bands of this native tribe often led raids against the Spaniards and other settlers in the Rio Grande Valley.*

Mesilla Valley, stopping under the cottonwoods and willows long enough to refresh their animals and fill their water jugs. The travelers hunted birds and ducks feeding on cattails at backwater pools, and turned out their animals to graze the brushlands near the river. From this green sanctuary they struck out on the Jornada del Muerto, the journey of death. (The Rio Grande once coursed through the Jornada, but by Oñate's time the high valley, some 25 miles wide and 90 miles long, was waterless desert.) They chanced this shortcut because at the north end of the Mesilla Valley the river cut through roller coaster terrain and a bosque impassable for the lumbering carretas, the wooden carts hauling their goods and supplies.

Thirst, however, was not their only worry on the 90-mile journey, for they knew that the mountains along the eastern flank of the Jornada harbored Mescalero Apaches. They knew, too, that more men had died from swift encounters with the Indians than from thirst. The fierce Mescaleros were relative newcomers to New Mexico, having been driven from the north to the marginal lands of southern New Mexico during the 1600s. Here they continued to practice their expert crafts of hunting and raiding. The dusty plumes sent up by the carretas showed the Mescaleros where to find goods to loot and horses to steal. At the same time, however, the annual procession of men and animals was a nagging reminder that their homelands were no longer their own. Desperately, fiercely, they fought back.

By the 1700s the royal highway was so overrun with mounted Apaches that travel was practically impossible. "Everyone travels at risk of his life," one missionary wrote, "for the heathen traverse them all being courageous and brave and they hurl themselves at danger like a people who know no God nor that there is any hell."

***Mescalero Apaches** used sumac and yucca to make their unique basketry. Their distinctive coiling technique resulted in baskets and trays that were flexible and thin-walled. This rare tray dates from about the turn of the century.*

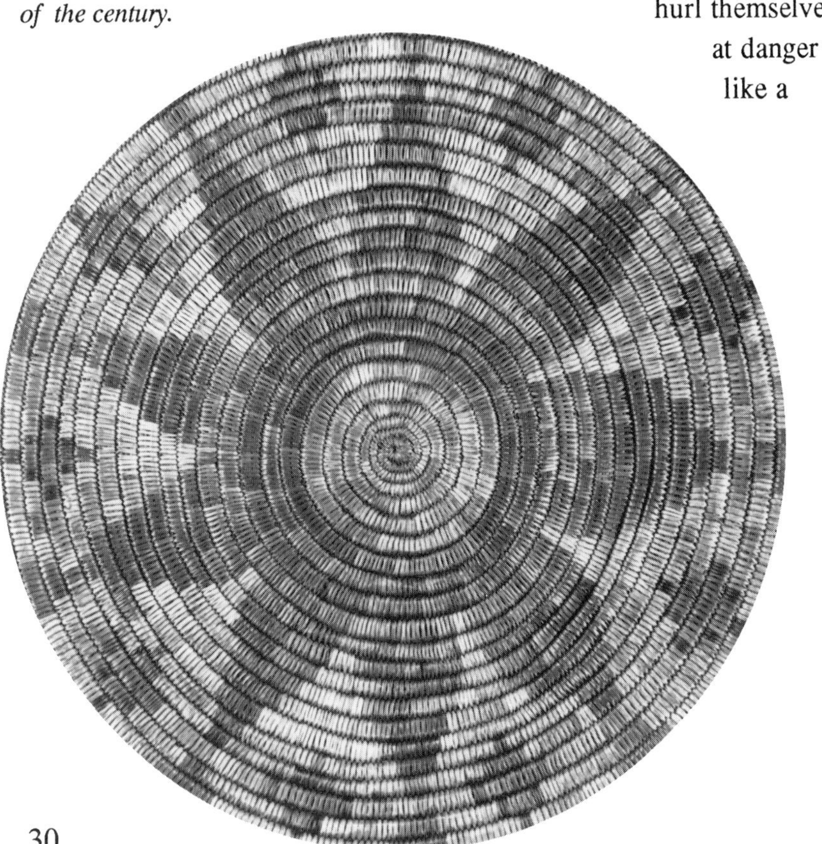

In 1810, after nearly a century of warfare, Spanish authorities and the Mescaleros entered into a treaty that granted the Indians rations and the right to occupy lands that included the Sacramento Mountains. During the relative peace of the 25-year truce, settlements along the trade route grew and prospered. El Paso, in particular, enjoyed the boom times brought about by the merchant traffic.

Spain's eagerness to make peace with the Mescaleros stemmed in part from a preoccupation with its own internal problems. Inflation and the tremendous costs of maintaining its far-flung empire had left Spain the weakest nation in Europe. Revolution was in the air. The Americans had wrested their freedom from England in 1776, the French from their monarchy in a bloodier version in 1789. The French cause had not gone unnoticed in Mexico where in 1810 in the town of Dolores lived a parish priest, who was known as a reformer and champion of the oppressed.

Miguel Hidalgo y Costilla had taken up the economic cause of the parish, introducing his Indian parishioners to industries such as tile making, wool weaving, beekeeping and wine making. During that time Father Hidalgo became associated with a "liter-

ary club,'' whose members discussed not literature but revolution. The conspirators plotted the separation of Mexico from Spain, planning to declare Mexico's independence on December 8, 1810, at the fair of San Juan de los Lagos.

However, when their plot was discovered, three of the rebels rode to warn Hidalgo, reaching the priest's house about two o'clock on the morning of the sixteenth of September. After hurried consultation they decided to call for independence at once. Hidalgo rang the church bells summoning his parishioners to mass early. To his congregation of Indians and mestizos, Hidalgo issued the *Grito de Dolores,* the ''cry'' for Mexican Independence.

Hidalgo, under the banner of the Virgin de Guadalupe, quickly proved a poor leader as his army of Indian foot soldiers soon became a mob. Within months he was captured by Spanish authorities and excuted before a firing squad. However, the war for independence lived on for another ten years.

With independence finally won in 1821, Mexico quickly freed New Mexico from its enforced isolation by opening its boundaries to outside trade. The next year American traders hauled their merchandise from Independence, Missouri, to Santa Fe to trade for gold, silver and furs. Soon, New Mexicans were buying goods from the Santa Fe traders and shipping them south on the Camino Real to sell in Chihuahua, Durango and Mexico City.

When the merchant wagons rolled through the mountain pass at El Paso del Norte (now Juárez), its citizens greeted the traders

El Paso del Norte, *what is known as Juárez today, became an important point of commerce on the trade route between Santa Fe and Chihuahua in the early 1800s. The distinctive church of Nuestra Señora de Guadalupe, depicted here in the early 1850s, was completed in 1659.*

The acequia madre *diverted water from the Rio Grande to the irrigable land in and near Las Cruces. The ditch, known by many names during its history, also supplied the water that operated the Las Cruces and the Barbaro Lucero and Son flour mills around the turn of the century.*

with eagerness and curiosity, offering for sale the produce of their orchards, fields and vineyards. Josiah Gregg, a trader and scholar, reported in 1839 that El Paso del Norte and its twin city, El Paso, on the east bank of the river had a combined population of some 4,000 people. The cities at the pass were becoming too crowded and the rich valley land too scarce. But up river land was plentiful and Mexico wanted to see it settled.

The Mexican government offered land grants to any group of at least 100 individuals who intented to establish a community on the grant. On Sept. 18, 1839, José Maria Costales and 115 men petitioned for such a grant. After a year of official inaction, they resubmitted their petition, this time saying approval of the Doña Ana Bend Colony Grant in the Mesilla Valley would alleviate suffering in the El Paso area. By then, however, the would-be colonists were too poor to make the move. Finally, in January 1843, Bernabé Montoya led 33 settlers (the others having abandoned the effort), to an area about five miles north of present day Las Cruces.

The hardship of living in the isolated colony quickly took its toll. When the military commander of the frontier, Gen. Mauricio Ugarte, made his first visit to the colony, only four people came to greet him. The others, he discovered, were hiding, too ashamed to reveal how poverty had reduced them to nakedness. Ugarte clothed the poor souls in soldiers' uniforms and gave them their first livestock, a horse and a mule.

By April all but 14 of the settlers had left. To prevent the colony from being abandoned, those remaining turned to the governor for help. They requested troops (sufficiently armed) to protect them from Indian attack, and a contingent of men to help them complete the irrigation ditch. For good measure, the colonists also requested exemption from military service and taxes.

The governor rushed a detachment of seven men to their aid, but advised the settlers that he could not, under law, exempt them from taxes or provide them with men to work on the ditch. Under the protection of the soldiers, the settlers, working only with crude wooden spades completed the *acequia madre* in April 1843, just in time for spring planting.

Centuries of both Indian and European tradition dictated the construction and use of the acequia madre, or main canal, which would bring water from the river to their crops. The acequia was community property and as such, was regulated by a municipal mayordomo, or ditch master. The rules were simple. A community member could use the ditch and its waters as long as he helped maintain the ditch and obeyed the rules of water use. Infractions, such as failure to close a ditch gate (which could

Giant yuccas *provide an imposing backdrop for James K. Livingston and William E. Baker (l-r) on the east side of the Organ Mountains in the area called "Palmilla Park." "I have always been grateful for the yucca, a plant without parallel in its lonely habitat of rocky slopes or arid plains, seldom blessed with rain, where it blooms in towering shafts of white-flowered beauty," wrote L.S.M. Curtain in her book* Healing Herbs of the Upper Rio Grande.

cause flood damage) resulted in charges for the damage and a one-peso fine for the offense.

The settlers had named their colony after Doña Ana, the legendary mistress of a vast rancho in the northern part of the valley. The title, according to custom, was attached to her name because she was a land owner. The mythical Doña Ana, it was told, had presided over orchards,

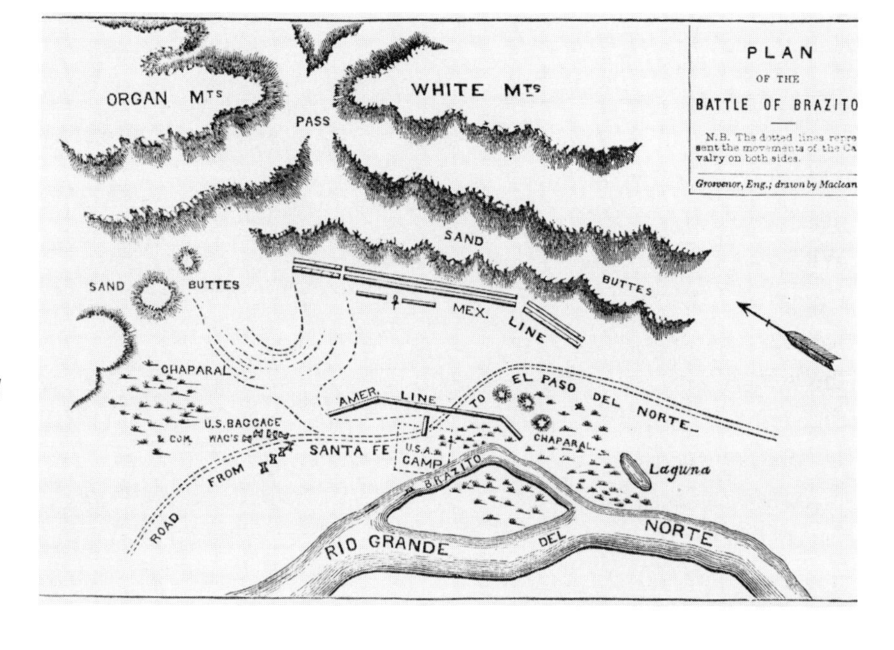

The Battle of Brazito was fought on Christmas Day in 1846 between Col. Alexander Doniphan's out-numbered Missouri Volunteers and Capt. Antonio Ponce de León's out-skilled Mexican forces. In less than an hour, Doniphan's men claimed victory in the only battle of the Mexican War fought in New Mexico.

vineyards, and fields of corn irrigated from the river, and herds of sheep on the nearby mesa. The settlers, by calling up her name, may have hoped to recreate the prosperous domain of the gentle woman. Perhaps they were right, for by the next January, 47 families and 22 single men, 261 people in all, made their home in the village of Doña Ana on the 35,000-acre grant.

The village was laid out according to Spanish custom, with the church and other public buildings facing a common plaza. But it was also designed for defense. The Mescaleros, at odds with their new Mexican rulers, made life impossible outside the protective limits of the larger settlements. With their hunting grounds confiscated and their game depleted, the Apaches again took to raiding the herds and settlements along the Rio Grande. This time around, they had guns. Soon, however, both the Mexican rule and the Apache terror would be broken by a stronger force under the banner of "manifest destiny."

John O'Sullivan, writing in a July 1845 issue of "United States Magazine," had given voice to what most Americans were

LATE DAY

The mountains lean long
into their shadows.
Somber, granite-carved.

Late day,
The earth is winding down
Hunkered against another night.

Alice W. Gruver

thinking. It was America's "manifest destiny," he wrote, "to overspread the continent . . . for the free development of our yearly multiplying millions." Within a year the United States Congress declared war on Mexico. Its reasons were many, but the primary one was to possess the continent from east to west.

News of war both pleased and alarmed the Santa Fe traders, including Missouri merchants who had been the loudest supporters of Manifest Destiny. They reasoned that if the Americans took New Mexico, the Missourians could control commerce at both ends of the Santa Fe Trail. But it was crucial that the takeover come about peacefully so as not to disrupt trade. As the American army marched toward Santa Fe, Missourian and Santa Fe trader James Magoffin was meeting secretly with Governor Manuel Armijo. President Polk had entrusted Magoffin with the task of convincing the governor to stand aside for the Americans. Possibly a bribe was offered as incentive.

Publicly Armijo issued a call to arms against the invaders, and with great bravado set up his defense at Apache Pass near Santa Fe. As the Americans drew near, however, Armijo suddenly abandoned the effort and fled to Mexico. When Col. Stephen Watts Kearny and his troops entered Santa Fe and took possession of New Mexico, they did so without firing a single shot.

In fact, the only battle in New Mexico took place at Brazito at a bend in the river just south of present day Las Cruces. In November 1846 Col. Alexander Doniphan and his Missouri Volunteers straggled into Doña Ana where for six weeks the village provided the force of more than 500 men with food and lodging. Then they marched south to meet the Mexican Army, as a parting gesture leaving the villagers a cannon to use against marauding Indians.

Doniphan's men were mostly farm boys who neither dressed nor acted like soldiers, but they were crack shots and fiercely loyal to their red-haired commander. By Christmas Day they had reached Brazito and were busy pitching camp while Doniphan and his staff played cards to see who should have a fine horse that had just been captured. However, Doniphan interrupted the game to assemble his men when in the distance dust signaled the arrival of some 1,000 Mexican troops. From the Mexican regiment rode a lone officer dressed in a splendid scarlet and blue uniform and bearing a black flag with skull and crossbones. The officer demanded that Doniphan come into the Mexican camp. Doniphan refused. The officer countered that they would come and get him, pointing to his black flag for emphasis. To which Doniphan's interpreter shouted, "Come on! They are ready for you."

And ready they were. The Mexicans, most of whom were poorly armed and trained, were no match for Doniphan's sharpshooters. When the half-hour battle was over, Doniphan had not lost a single man and listed only seven wounded, while the Mexicans counted 63 dead, 172 wounded and some 300 missing. The battle won, Doniphan and his fellow gamblers returned to their cards, realizing only after the game that the prize horse had escaped during the battle.

The Treaty of Guadalupe Hidalgo ended the war in 1848, and ceded the lands east of the Rio Grande, including those of the Doña Ana colony, to the United States. By then, Doña Ana was swarming with Americans, including Texans who were claiming rights to undeeded land under a secret treaty Mexico had made with the Republic of Texas years earlier. (To uncomplicate the matter, Congress in 1850 paid the Texans $10,000 to withdraw their claims.) Also, many of the

families saw the entry of the Americans as a threat to the way of life they had known for generations under Spanish and Mexican rule. With assistance from the Mexican government and under the persuasive guidance of Father Ramón Ortiz, these families were relocated south of Doña Ana in areas that remained under Mexican control. Meanwhile, the residents of Doña Ana appealed to Pablo Melendres, their justice of the peace, to do something about the overcrowding. Acting as the village spokesman, Melendres petitioned the U.S. government to lay out a separate town to accommodate the eager newcomers.

The site chosen lay six miles south of the village near an old historic burial ground, known by all who passed by. Susan Magoffin, the young wife of Santa Fe trader Sam Magoffin, recalled the site's dark history in her January 1847 diary entry. "Yesterday we passed over the spot where a few years since a party of the Apaches attacked Gen. Armijo as he returned from the Pass with a party of troops, and killed some fourteen of his men, the graves of whom, marked by a rude cross, are now seen. . . ." The crosses would give the new town its name.

The Organ Mountains *may have been mined as early as 1798 by Padre Phillippe La Rue, a French nobleman and member of the Franciscan Order. Mining later emerged in the early 1850s, as illustrated here, and was a profitable yet primitive venture.*

M
54

Farms and Forts

1849 - 1880

There is no country protected by our flag
and subject to our laws so little known
to the people of the United States
than New Mexico.

Capt. W.W.H. Davis, *El Gringo*

When the U.S. Army sent Lt. Delos Bennett Sackett to lay out the new town in 1849, he found 120 eager Las Crucens camped out in brush shelters on what later would be the city's plaza. The families waited patiently, talking in small groups while the lieutenant's assistants, using nothing more accurate than a rawhide rope, marked off the city's new streets. When they finished they collected their maps and papers and under the big cottonwoods near what is now Griggs Street, set up for the drawing. One by one, and then in twos and threes, the heads of families gathered under the shade trees. Then, each in turn drew a suerte from a hat. The suerte, which means chance or luck, determined which property the family would own. It was a lucky day indeed.

Although it was an American town, laid out along Sackett's imprecise grid, early Las Cruces had the honeycombed look of its pueblo predecessors. Its houses, courtyards and corrals, each one seemingly connected to another, were crowded against dusty streets. No wonder the Indians hesitated to raid the corrals, for who dared chance getting trapped in this one-story maze.

Their rectangular homes were simple, practical dwellings of coarse adobe bricks. The bricks were a mixture of mud and straw (the dirt streets being a handy source of mud until a court order curtailed the practice), patted into shape and dried in the sun. Because wood was scarce, adobe was used to build everything from houses to baking ovens to corrals. The only wood found in these early homes were in the

***Dancers** (previous pages) of the Ballet Folklorico de la Tierra del Encanto truly enchant the crowd at the Cinco de Mayo fiesta on Mesilla's plaza. Mesilla celebrates this Mexican national holiday every May, reconfirming its traditional ties to Mexico.*

St. Genevieve's, *constructed in 1859, served as Las Cruces' first church under the direction of Father Manuel Chávez. The church is pictured here around the turn of the century, surrounded by the homes and businesses of that time.*

Lt. Delos Bennett Sackett, *(right) commander of 100 men in the U.S. cavalry at Doña Ana, surveyed the original townsite of Las Cruces in 1849. Sackett was later to become a brigadier general and served as inspector general in 1866 with responsibility of investigating and reporting on the "protection of the routes across the continent to the Pacific from molestation by hostile Indians."*

Jacal construction, *(below) which preceded the use of adobe bricks, was still a common method of building at the end of the nineteenth century. The walls of the jacal were made from branches and brush, which were then plastered with mud. This late 1800s photograph shows homes made with the combined use of adobe and jacal methods.*

door and window frames and in vigas, the cottonwood logs used as roof supports. Poorer residents, to whom wood was a luxury, often lived in houses with only one door and no windows at all. Others lived in jacales, the mud plastered timber and brush dwellings like those of their ancestors.

Life in early Las Cruces was carried on mostly outdoors. The men worked on outlying farms where they grew grapes, chile, corn and beans. The women tended vegetable gardens that defined the village's western limits at Water St. The gardens were irrigated from the adjacent acequia madre, the "mother" ditch that tapped into the Rio Grande. Much of the household activity took place in the walled courtyard behind the house where mothers baked bread in open air hornos, beehive shaped adobe ovens and their children chased chickens and goats. Other livestock was kept in an adjoining corral where high adobe walls discouraged trespassers.

Village life also included a lively mix of soldiers, military suppliers, freighters, and traders following the Chihuahua Trail to Santa Fe. Hotels and bars were popular stops, while general stores provided supplies and dry goods for residents as well as travelers.

One of these proprietors was Martin Amador, or rather his enterprising mother, Gregoria Rodela de Amador. In 1850 the young widow from Juárez opened a store

***Before the railroad** brought changes in transportation, Martin Amador's successful business of hauling freight between Santa Fe and Chihuahua enabled him to settle in Las Cruces and raise his family. Martin's wife, Refugio, and some of their sons and daughters are pictured above in the late 1890s. They are (l-r, front row) Emelia, Martin, Refugio, and John; (back row) Julieta, Maria, Frank, Clotilde, and Corina.*

on the corner of what is now Main St. and Amador Ave. to make a living for her three young children, including 11-year-old Martin. She sold supplies to soldiers and citizens alike. To ensure that young Martin learned English, she sent him to work for Col. George Hayward at Fort Fillmore where he earned $6 a month and eventually a commission for trading at the post. He later broadened his business experience by taking the position of paymaster at the Bennett Mine in the Organ Mountains. During this time Martin expanded his mother's enterprise to include a

Many buildings *(right) in early Las Cruces were constructed with mud adobe bricks. In the late 1800s a caption on an Atchison, Topeka & Santa Fe Railroad photograph described these adobe buildings as having an appearance of impending dissolution. "One could wish that anything so obtrusive might possess at least an attribute of beauty, but not one has the adobe house." Today adobe homes are sought and prized by discerning dwellers.*

Women's work *(far right) in turn-of-the-century Las Cruces was very similar to that of their rural counterparts. Animals and gardens required tending, and water for washing was still drawn from a well. This woman was photographed just a few blocks from St. Genevieve's Catholic Church.*

freight hauling business and sleeping rooms for his teamsters.

In 1859 the good citizens of Las Cruces built their first church on the four city lots reserved under Lt. Sackett's plan. The new church, a one-story adobe, was named St. Genevieve for the young heroine who had saved Paris from the Huns. Father Manuel Chávez was its first priest. In 1863 for the first time the heavy tones of church bells could be heard calling parishioners to daily mass. The two small bells that hung above the church entrance had been cast from metal, jewelry and coins gathered from around town.

These homemade, hometown bells were thought to be mysteriously lost when the new bells were installed in 1904. Years later, however, it was discovered that the old broken bells simply had been sent in trade to the St. Louis foundry that made the new bells.

The year after Las Cruces was founded, another group of Doña Ana residents established Mesilla, a few miles west, on the Mexican side of the river. Although the two appeared to be kindred villages, Mesilla was a Mexican town, founded by families who looked to the Catholic church for spiritual authority and the Mexican government for political leadership. Here in Mexican territory, they believed they would find a haven from land-hungry Texans, the United States government, and Apaches. They were to be proved wrong on all counts.

In the 1850s, Mesilla was showing early signs of prosperity. Doña Ana County was formed in 1852, with Mesilla as the county seat. The expansive county stretched from California to Texas and by 1855 included nearly one-third of present day Arizona and New Mexico. Farming also prospered during that period. Justice of the Peace Rafael Ruelas reported "abundant harvests" of 320 bushels of grain despite a great drought. Silt left by the meandering Rio Grande had proved as rich and fertile as the farmers had hoped. By 1853 valley farms were producing 25,000 bushels of corn, 7,500 bushes of wheat and 5,000 bushels of beans a year.

The Indians took note of the valley's abundance under the new colonists, particularly the farms and corrals of Mesilla. In one early morning raid, Apaches quietly stole into the village and with a strip of wet rawhide sawed through an adobe corral and silently led away 15 horses.

While settlers in the Mesilla Valley were occupied with the business of farming and defending against the Indians, events both east and west soon would intrude on their lives. The year Las Cruces was founded, 80,000 "forty-niners" had flocked to California's newly discovered gold fields.

Shortly after *the signing of the Treaty of Guadalupe Hidalgo in 1848, colonists from El Paso del Norte, Doña Ana, and elsewhere began to settle in Mesilla. The town grew and prospered from its central location between San Diego, California, and San Antonio, Texas.*

***The Butterfield Overland Mail** stage stopped in Mesilla to pick up mail, passengers, and fresh horses on its westward route to Fort Cummings. Passengers waited for the coach in what is now the dining room of the El Patio Restaurant. This drawing by Bob Diven depicts the stage in Mesilla before the Civil War.*

In 1851 prospectors searching for the "Lost Padre Mine" established the first mine in Doña Ana County. Legend has it that in 1798 a dying soldier told a French priest of gold buried in the Organ Mountains. Padre LaRue and his followers secretly mined this rich vein until the Catholic church discovered his little enterprise. To prevent authorities from taking the gold, the padre covered the mine's entrance. When LaRue was murdered, the location of the mine was lost with him.

Although Doña Ana's first mine (which was owned by former California Volunteer Hugh Stephenson) was neither the Lost Padre Mine nor full of gold, it yielded lead and $70,000 worth of silver. However, better prospects in the silver mines of western New Mexico and the Civil War soon cooled the mining fever.

In 1853 a railroad survey showed that if the United States wanted a southern railroad route to the Pacific, it had to cross Mexican territory. That year a South Carolina railroad executive named James Gadsden was appointed minister to Mexico. Gadsden, a proponent of the southern route, arrived to find the Mexican government of Antonio Santa Anna on the verge of bankruptcy. The savvy Gadsden had the perfect solution to Santa Anna's financial woes--sell part

of its northern territories to the United States. Santa Anna agreed. After considerable debate, the U.S. Senate ratified the Gadsden Treaty on April 25, 1854, in which the United States purchased from Mexico a 30,000 square-mile strip of land from south of the Gila River to the present Mexican border for $10 million. The treaty secured much more than a railroad route, for within the Gadsden Purchase was the fertile Mesilla Valley and the rich copper lode at Santa Rita.

The residents of Mesilla ceremoniously witnessed the end of Mexican rule when the American flag was raised over their plaza on Nov. 16, 1854. Although they had eluded American citizenship in 1848, few of them decided to leave once again. These reluctant Americans did not realize it then, but Mesilla was about to enter its golden age.

During this period, Mesilla had already surpassed Las Cruces as the valley's transportation and economic crossroads. Oñate's old route north through Las Cruces had lost importance as adventurers now passed through Mesilla seeking fortunes to the west. With the coming of the railroad still nearly three decades away, New York stage line owner John Butterfield saw the opportunity to fill the transportation gap for these western wayfarers. Butterfield's ambitious plan was to carry mail and passengers from St. Louis to San Francisco in 25 days or less. In 1857, the U.S. government awarded him an annual subsidy of $600,000 to do just that.

For $200 a passenger could make this 2,700-mile trip in one of Butterfield's canvas-topped stages. Day and night the stage rolled onward, stopping every 20 miles to change mule teams and to allow passengers their three meals a day (not included in the fare). On Sept. 30, 1858, the first west-bound stage reached Mesilla by way of El Paso and a ferry crossing a mile and a half below the village where the Rio Grande was but "an insignificant puddle." Two years later summer rains would turn the crossing into a wild river 400 feet wide and 12 feet deep.

The Mesilla station, the largest between El Paso and Los Angeles, consisted of a high walled corral attached to a large adobe building located just "south of Fountain's new store and post office." Here passengers were warmly greeted and quickly fed, perhaps the "omnipresent chili" reported by one traveler. One Butterfield passenger, New York Times reporter Waterman L. Ormsby, observed that "A few speculating Yankees live here (Mesilla) and are making fortunes rapidly. . . ." The enterprising businessmen, he wrote, were asking high prices for everything "except grain and

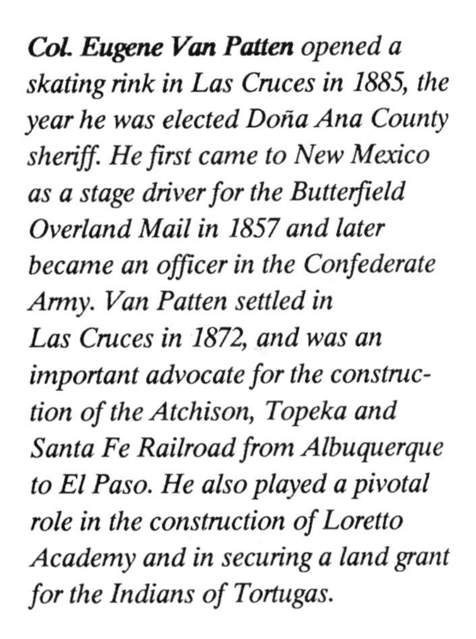

Col. Eugene Van Patten *opened a skating rink in Las Cruces in 1885, the year he was elected Doña Ana County sheriff. He first came to New Mexico as a stage driver for the Butterfield Overland Mail in 1857 and later became an officer in the Confederate Army. Van Patten settled in Las Cruces in 1872, and was an important advocate for the construction of the Atchison, Topeka and Santa Fe Railroad from Albuquerque to El Paso. He also played a pivotal role in the construction of Loretto Academy and in securing a land grant for the Indians of Tortugas.*

hay which are comparatively cheap."

By 1860 Mesilla had more than 2,000 residents, while the village of Las Cruces had less than half that number. Albuquerque, with 1,760 people, and tiny El Paso with 428, gave no hint of their future importance to the Southwest. That year Mesilla was made the junction for the Butterfield Overland Mail route to Santa Fe, but by the next spring this route was suspended. By summer, the Civil War had reached the Mesilla Valley.

By and large New Mexicans took little interest in the causes of slavery and states rights that had split the nation. Territorial New Mexico had been established in 1850 with only brief mention of slavery. The official record stated that when the territory is admitted as a state it "shall be received into the Union, with or without slavery" depending upon the articles of New Mexico's constitution at the time of admission.

At the beginning of the Civil War, only about twenty slaves

lived in New Mexico, most of them servants of military officers. States rights had little appeal to a territory who wanted to become part of the Union, not separate from it. One New Mexican summed up the territory's position on succession saying, "She desires to be let alone . . . no interference from one side or the other. . . ."

Indifference alone did not keep New Mexico out of the national debate. Since the landing of Cortés, New Mexico had operated a system of peonage and Indian slavery to meet its labor needs. Under indebted servitude, poor laborers, peons, were given wage advances and were required by law to remain with their employer until the debt was paid. At wages of $5 a month, many peons were bound to years of servitude during their productive years. At the same time, employers incurred no obligation to care for the peon in old age or to maintain his family. New Mexico's arid climate and the predominance of subsistence agriculture also made it a poor market for slave labor.

Attorney W.W.H. Davis, who lived in New Mexico in 1857 observed, "The only practical difference between (peonage) and negro slavery is, that the peons are not bought and sold in the market as chattels; but in other respects I believe the difference is in favor of the negro."

In 1866, the New Mexico legislature (in an obvious attempt to please Congress and improve its status for statehood) repealed the restrictive Free Negro law, and amended 'the Peon law' to make servitude *voluntary.* In 1867, the year Congress abolished the peonage system, the territory had an estimated 1,500 to 3,000 Indian slaves and an unknown count of indebted peons.

The Confederates viewed New Mexico solely as a supply route from California where they had hopes of establishing a coastal port. To carry out their plan, they enlisted the support of sympathizers, particularly in southern New Mexico. The southern part of the state was inhabited by a sympathetic corps of ranchers and merchants, many of them former Texans, who had moved to the Mesilla Valley after the Gadsden Purchase. Feeling they had little in common with the Hispanic-oriented northern counties and that they were neglected by the authorities in Santa Fe, the new settlers pushed to form a separate territory. In March 1861, residents of Tucson and Mesilla held separate conventions and voted to join the Confederacy.

Four months later, Lt. Col. John R. Baylor, a Texas lawyer and Indian fighter, led 300 Texans north from El Paso into New Mexico, leisurely marching into Mesilla on July 25 where the Confederates were "received with every manifestation of joy" according to the fledgling *Mesilla Times*. Decidedly sympathetic to the Confederate cause, the newspaper went on to report that the "overjoyed" citizens offered the troops forage and supplies,

***Fort Fillmore** was established about six miles south of Las Cruces in 1851. The fort served as a U.S. Army outpost for ten years but was abandoned after the Confederacy was welcomed into the Mesilla Valley.*

declaring themselves "weary of Yankee tyranny and oppression."

Six miles to the south lay Fort Fillmore, a Union outpost with some 500 "well-drilled" soldiers, 100 women and children, and a commander who possessed a "pale face and cowardly soul." Maj. Isaac Lynde led his troops with "majestic indifference," according to the post medical officer.

After a brief skirmish at Mesilla where Baylor's riflemen sent the Union troops into confusion, Lynde hurried them back to Fort Fillmore. There Lynde directed his men to destroy the fort's supplies of medicine, equipment and liquor. Abandoning the garrison in the middle of the night, Lynde's troops started the long retreat to Fort Stanton. The next morning when Baylor spotted the telltale column of dust leading toward the Organ Mountains, he set off in pursuit. There was no rush. The Union soldiers, having rescued the whiskey from destruction, suffered miserably under the hot morning sun. For five miles, Baylor reported, the road was "lined with the fainting, famished soldiers, who threw down their arms as we passed and begged for water."

At San Augustin Springs, Lynde enjoyed a comfortable lunch as his officers drew up their men to meet Baylor's force. When the Texans advanced to within 300 yards of the Union line, Lynde sent out a flag of truce, and over the protests of all his officers, surrendered. From his headquarters in Mesilla, the victorious Baylor then proclaimed New Mexico from about Socorro south as part of the Confederate Territory of Arizona and named himself its military governor.

By the next spring, however, the Confederates had won only poor victories in New Mexico. Their supplies destroyed and the countryside hostile, the ragtag army retreated down the Rio Grande destined for San Antonio, Texas.

The brash Col. Baylor also had worn out his welcome. He and *Mesilla Times* editor R.P. Kelley had a falling out over a series of articles Kelley had written criticizing Baylor as having an "incapacity" for his duties. Finally when Kelley accused Baylor of "probable cowardice and corruption," Baylor had enough. The editor's Bowie knife was no match for the colonel's pistol. Kelley died of a gunshot wound to the neck, Baylor was "triumphantly acquitted" of the crime, and the paper's publisher, W.C. Murray, abandoned his press to join the Confederate evacuation.

Coincidently Gen. James H. Carleton and 2,300 Union volunteers were marching from California to drive the Confederates from New Mexico. By the time they reached the Rio Grande on Aug. 10, 1862, the rebel army had left.

The Californians were welcomed with enthusiastic celebration. Merchants reopened their doors. Residents unearthed hidden caches of champagne. "Balls and dinners," one soldier wrote, "were all the rage." Unlike the Texans, the California troops had volunteered as much for the adventure and excitement of seeing new places as they had for the soldier's pay and the Union cause.

With the rebels gone, the Californians spent most of their time fighting hostile Indians and enjoying the pleasures of the Mesilla Valley, which one soldier wrote included hunting, fishing, swimming in the Rio Grande and "basking in the sunny smiles of the 'Castilian beauties' of Mesilla."

Although the Civil War had brought a measure of hardship to the valley, the influx of soldiers, particularly the California Column, also brought government contracts, growth, and a certain liveliness to Mesilla and Las Cruces. With Fort Fillmore having been abandoned in 1862, the U.S. Army rented quarters in both towns to house its troops.

The soldiers were very visible members of the Las Cruces community, which by 1863 had grown to 800 souls. The 215 enlisted men assigned to Las Cruces were quartered in large adobe buildings on the city's broad dusty main street. One official report describes their

OLD MESILLA

That heat has passed and slowly beats the heart
Of Old Mesilla, standing from the modern ways
apart,
No sounds are heard about the sleepy square
Except the sound of mocking birds, the sighing of
the summer air;
But through the dreams, Mesilla still holds fast
Against her breast the relics of her memorized past.

Margaret Page Hood

accommodations as "rude and uncomfortable, with earthen floors, and frequently without window frames or sashes." The troops used the sun-baked plaza in front of St. Genevieve's Catholic Church as a parade ground where they practiced military drills.

While the Union army was preoccupied with the Civil War, the Indians were again free to raid the territory's outlying settlements with impunity. After a report of yet another Apache raid wiping out a ranch family, the exasperated editor of the *Mesilla Miner* pleaded, "How long, Oh! how long are we to endure these horrible outrages? . . . Will Congress never give us protection?" Not until 1863.

By then the Confederates had gone and General Carleton had been left with thousands of soldiers scattered throughout the territory who were ready for action. The general soon came up with a plan to use the troops to solve the "Indian problem." He believed a combination of merciless warfare and destruction of their food supply would quickly subdue the Indians. Once subjugated, he proposed confining them on reservations where they would be taught Christianity and farming. He tested his strategy first against the Mescaleros. By March 1863, the campaign was completed and Carlton brought 400 warriors with their families to the new Bosque Redondo Reservation on the Pecos River. The Navajos were next. Government troops marched through Navajo settlements, destroying

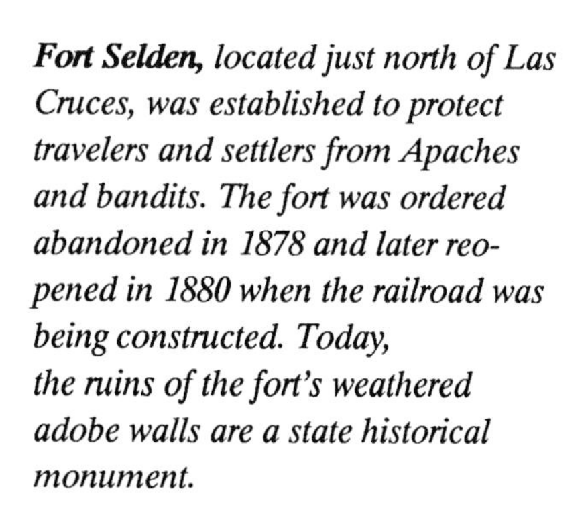
Fort Selden, *located just north of Las Cruces, was established to protect travelers and settlers from Apaches and bandits. The fort was ordered abandoned in 1878 and later reopened in 1880 when the railroad was being constructed. Today, the ruins of the fort's weathered adobe walls are a state historical monument.*

***Black infantry** regiments occupied Fort Selden, after its construction in 1867. This drawing by Bob Diven depicts a black trooper, or "buffalo" soldier as the Indians would have called him, scouting the area near the post, which is pictured in the distance, east of the Rio Grande at the foot of Robledo Mountain.*

crops and orchards, and capturing huge flocks of sheep. Within months the Navajos, exhausted and starving, surrendered. With their submission, both tribes--traditional enemies--were confined to the Bosque Redondo. The Mescaleros, miserable in their captivity, one by one and family by family slipped away into the mountains to the south.

Gradually the Mescaleros, starving and tired of fighting, gathered in greater numbers near Fort Stanton where they knew they would receive rations. In 1873 the government created a reservation for the Mescaleros on the eastern slopes of the White and Sacramento mountains. In 1849, nearly 3,000 Mescaleros inhabited New Mexico. But by 1888, their numbers had been reduced to 431.

One of Carleton's Indian fighting forts was established in 1865 on the banks of the Rio Grande 15 miles north of Las Cruces where the river "teemed with beaver" and cottonwoods grew in thick stands. Fine grazing land lay nearby. Fort Selden, with its ubiquitous flat-roofed adobe buildings, was a "dull little place" according to one officer's wife who spent a brief tour there. The soldiers thought so, too. Despite its location between the Mescalero and Mimbres Apaches, its troops saw very little action. Life there was a string of monotonous duties and

John Martin *came to the Mesilla Valley in 1861 as a lieutenant with the First California Infantry. He married in 1865 and settled in Fort Selden, where he operated a ferry across the Rio Grande. In 1867 Martin successfully struck water on the Jornada del Muerto and became known as "Jack Martin, the Chief of the Jornada." He is pictured here in the 1870s.*

The church walls *at Bosque Seco, which was located about eight miles south of Las Cruces, were made of unplastered adobe. The church was constructed in a typical architectural style, with vigas and a latilla ceiling. Shown here at the turn of the century, this structure has long since eroded away.*

drills. The nearest town was a "rough spot" called Leasburg, which was quickly placed off-limits.

For one-third of its history, Fort Selden was garrisoned by black troops. Nearly 180,000 blacks had served in the Union army during the Civil War, and when the war ended, four black regiments were sent west under white commissioned officers to fight Indians and guard settlers. Gen. William T. Sherman praised these troops, saying "they make first-rate sentinels, are faithful to their trust and are as brave as the occasion calls for."

By 1884 Fort Selden had become so peaceful that fort commander Capt. Arthur MacArthur's two young sons chased lizards across roads where two decades earlier Indians had terrorized wagon trains. Douglas MacArthur, one of the lizard-hunting brothers, eventually went on to become a general and the American commander in the Philippines during World War II.

In the second half of the 19th century the federal government spent millions of dollars furnishing the Army of the West with food, clothing, livestock and other supplies. Military posts like Fort Selden were a ready market for local grain and hay. In 1865, for example, local merchant Epifanio Aguirre received $138,000 for transporting supplies to the army in New Mexico. Agents such as Henry Lesinsky of Las Cruces and Warren Shedd at San Augustin Springs prospered supplying the government with goods ranging from bacon, to cattle, to flour and charcoal.

Army-built roads, which connected their military posts, also were used by civilians. In 1876 the army completed a military telegraph line linking Santa Fe, Las Cruces and Mesilla to the Arizona-San Diego military line. When the army ran out of money during construction, private citizens eagerly contributed the funds to complete the line. Local supplier John Martin provided the telegraph poles at $1.75 apiece. When the line between Las Cruces and Santa Fe was completed in April of that year, residents of both towns celebrated, with the Mesilla brass band leading the festivities.

Most of those who settled the Mesilla Valley before the war lived on small subsistence farms, where success largely depended upon the vagaries of the river. In 1865 the Rio Grande swept through the valley, its floodwaters scouring away its banks and cutting a new course to the west. When the floodwaters subsided Mesilla found itself now to the east of the river, with only muddy bottom land separating it from Las Cruces. About every ten summers the river also went dry, forcing farmers to abandon their parched fields. One group

The enterprising Numa Reymond *became one of the wealthiest, most prominent citizens of Las Cruces after establishing the first express company in the Mesilla Valley in 1869. Reymond was one of the founders of the Las Cruces College (now New Mexico State University) and was a member of its first board of regents.*

Emelia Van Patten *was the strikingly beautiful daughter of Eugene Van Patten and his wife, Benita Madrid Vargas. Mrs. Van Patten was a Piro Indian descendant of the Indians who migrated from the Guadalupe Mission in El Paso to Tortugas. Cross-cultural marriages were an established part of society, particularly after the Civil War.*

of farmers became so disgusted with the unruly river that they packed up and moved east of the Organ Mountains. There they founded the village of Tularosa, named for the small, civilized river flowing from the Sacramento Mountains.

Newcomers who came to Las Cruces after the Civil War entered the life of the community as merchants, craftsmen, miners and lawyers. The Las Cruces of 1870 counted several Texans and a smattering of southerners among its 1,200 some residents. They soon were joined by a lone Chinese laborer and several German immigrants, many of them Jews. When Samuel J. Freudenthal moved to Las Cruces, he was part of a wave of Jewish merchants who played a major role in bringing economic progress to New Mexico. Here he joined his cousin Henry Lesinsky (and a slew of other relatives) in the business of buying grain from local farmers and selling it to the government.

The California Column also contributed its share of entrepreneurs to the Las Cruces economy. The three-year enlistment of many of the Californians ended during the fall of 1864. Unlike nearly every other regiment, these volunteer soldiers could chose between leaving the service at their last place of duty or returning to California for discharge. Those who found the territory harsh and monotonous, left for California or accepted posts in eastern units. Others, however, found life in the valley pleasant, the people friendly and the opportunities promising.

Those "sunny smiles" also proved compelling. The 1870 census shows that of the 89 unmarried veterans of the California Column who stayed on in Mew Mexico after their discharge, 79 married or were living with Hispanic women. Not only was the beauty of the Hispanic women an asset, so were their ties to Hispanic society and land ownership. For many of the women, marriage to an Anglo also meant a rise in social status, primarily because the educational levels and incomes of the Anglos were higher than those of Hispanic men. While not all matches were perfect, descendants of these cross-cultural marriages continue to play an important role in defining Southern New Mexico's culture.

John D. Barncastle, like most Anglo men in Las Cruces during that time, was married to a Hispanic woman. His wife, Josefa, the daughter of Pablo Melendrez, inherited her father's lands. By 1880, the former Union sergeant owned a store, a flour mill, a 700-acre farm and a profitable vineyard. He was among the first farmers to plant pecan and pomegranate trees and to experiment with raising teas.

John Martin (the telegraph pole supplier) also had a talent for finding water. In 1867 he successfully sank a 164-foot well midway on the Jornada del Muerto. At the little oasis, he and his wife, Esther, operated a hotel, which also served as a stage stop, government forage agency, post office and headquarters for their small cattle ranch.

At least a dozen California veterans, including William L. Rynerson and Joseph F. Bennett, staked claims in the Organs in the two decades after their discharge from the army. While Bennett focused his energies mostly on his successful mining company, Rynerson's wide-ranging interests were dominated by politics.

The far-sighted William L. Rynerson had bought property in Las Cruces even before his discharge. By 1880 he owned 180 acres of good farm land (valued at $10,000) where he employed a corn planter and hay baler, the latest in farm equipment. Rynerson's real talent, however, was politics. "The Tall Sycamore of the Rio Grande" served three successive terms in the territorial council, where he kept a watchful eye on events that might affect Las Cruces.

In 1878 the first railroad steamed across the Raton Pass into New Mexico, and within the next 30 months construction crews had completed the line south to El Paso. There the Santa

Fe Railroad would link up with the westbound tracks of the Southern Pacific Railroad. Like many western railroads, the Santa Fe Railroad, in its race to the Pacific, was building track faster than it could pay for it. The towns in the railway's path, however, saw the railroad as a giant corporation and were stunned to find the railroad asking *them* for money. When railroad officials approached Mesilla for a right-of-way, the land owners refused to sell, perhaps holding out for a higher price. The railroad then decided to bypass Mesilla for a more charitable neighbor, just as it had bypassed Santa Fe and Bernalillo in favor of Albuquerque.

That lesson was not lost on Rynerson and his partners in the Las Cruces Town Company, Isidoro Armijo, Henry J. Cuniffe and Simon B. Newcomb. Combining their assets and talents, the men offered the railroad donated land for both a depot and a right of way through Las Cruces. Their generous offer was accepted.

Bearded William L. Rynerson *was a prudent entrepreneur, successful politician and prominent attorney. Rynerson came to the Mesilla Valley as a California Volunteer during the Civil War. and, like others, remained to make Las Cruces his home. Also pictured here in the late 1890s are Katie Lemon (standing), Luciana Lemon Rynerson, and the two Rynerson boys.*

The Great Civilizer

1881 - 1911

New Library

The Las Cruces band is progressing rapidly under the leadership of professor Antonio Ruiz and will soon be ready to entertain our citizens with their plaza concerts.

Las Cruces Citizen, May 10, 1902

By mid-afternoon on April 26, 1881, a noisy mixture of people had gathered at the end of what is now Las Cruces Avenue to celebrate the arrival of the first train to Las Cruces. Everyone from old men in sombreros to an assortment of children and dogs had crowded near the tracks, eager for the "grand jollification," reported the semi-weekly newspaper *Thirty-four.* Some had come in from outlying villages, while others simply walked the few blocks from town to the new wooden depot.

At four o'clock dignitaries in starched collars and ladies in tight waisted taffetas collected on the train platform to greet the "great civilizer." As the whole town watched, young ladies with baskets of flowers sprinkled roses and pansies on the tracks before the oncoming train.

After many speeches by those of "great repute," the tracks were christened with wine and the festivities commenced. By now the engine and the railroad employees had been draped in flower garlands courtesy of the young flower girls. Further hospitality (in the form of several wagon loads of wine) was extended to workman and citizen alike. The newspaper reported that "business was almost entirely suspended and everybody turned out and had a good time."

Whether the "great civilizer" lived up to its billing during the first decades after it steamed across the West is disputable. What is certain, is that it brought change and it brought it quickly. In the ten years after the railroad entered Albuquerque, its population tripled to 6,000 people. The link-up between the Southern

The new library *(previous pages) at New Mexico State University was completed in 1992 at a cost of $11.1 million. The college's first library was a reading room where patrons could be in "communion with the greatest and best minds of all ages past."*

Pacific and the Atchison, Topeka and Santa Fe railroads at El Paso doubled that city's 1,500 population in a single month. By 1890, El Paso was a Wild West town of 8,000 people.

Las Cruces, unlike Albuquerque and El Paso, was neither terminus nor crossroads for the railroad. During the 1880s, its population grew from 1,575 to only 2,300. Nevertheless, the railroad brought change to nearly every social and economic aspect of life in the Mesilla Valley.

Established businesses were among the first to benefit from the influx of travelers to Las Cruces. Martin Amador who, before the coming of the railroad, had built his fortune hauling freight, now used the railroad to market agricultural products and

***The Rio Grande Hotel** (above) in 1887 charged its guests two dollars a day to sleep in one of its 14 rooms, eat a good meal in its dining room, and board a horse in its corral.*

***Train passengers** (below) arriving at the Las Cruces station in 1901 were met by the horse-drawn carriages of Amador's Passenger Company. The construction of the railroad, which was originally planned to go through Mesilla, brought opportunity and prosperity to Las Cruces and the Mesilla Valley.*

handle deliveries from mail order houses. He converted his former teamster stop into "the finest hotel in Las Cruces!" The adobe building also served as a county courthouse, post office and jail. Its large central room was sometimes used as a theater. Drivers for the Amador and its competitor, the Don Bernardo Hotel, often raced their omnibuses to be the first to meet passengers on incoming trains.

***Shalam** was a Utopian colony established six miles northwest of Las Cruces on land purchased from John D. Barncastle in 1884. Dr. John B. Newbrough and Andrew M. Howland founded the Faithist Colony, which cared for orphaned and abandoned children until it closed in 1907.*

One morning in 1884 the passengers included a most unusual man on a most unusual mission. John Newbrough had come to establish a Utopian society in the Mesilla Valley. Newbrough had been a dentist in Cleveland, Ohio, when in 1849, he left to join the Gold Rush. Remarkably, he struck it rich, sending a fortune in bagged gold dust and small nuggets to his mother for safekeeping. Then he went to Australia where he amassed a second fortune in the gold fields. His future secure, Newbrough then turned to his true calling--helping the downtrodden.

By study and practice he became a mystic with strange powers. In about 1880, Newbrough said an angel directed him to find a typewriter. For the next fifty weeks he said the angel guided his hands while he typed *Oahspe,* the book that provided the blueprint for founding Shalam Colony.

Legend has it that in 1884 Newbrough and his friend Andrew M. Howland came to Las Cruces and led by spirit guides, drove blindfolded to a lonely bend of the Rio Grande a few miles north of town. There they established Shalam Colony. The Utopian colony would be a place where people could grow their own food and live righteous and dedicated lives away from the sins of the cities. Shalam also would serve as a home for foundlings and orphans.

Newbrough recruited a hundred laborers from Doña Ana at a dollar a day to build 35 structures, including a 42-room Fraternum. Once the building were completed, Newbrough brought in the babies. The first ten, all less than six months old, and most ill and undernourished, traveled to Shalam from New Orleans in a chartered Pullman car. Their education began in infancy with religious instruction and by the time they were school age, they could write, memorize and act out lengthy, moralizing spirit plays. They learned to play the piano, and to draw and paint. The children ate two meals a day, the first at 4:30 a.m., and went to bed, as did everyone, at 6:00 p.m.

Newbrough died in 1891 and his Utopian dream began to unravel. The expenses of Shalam's huge farming enterprise began to exceed its profits. The Shalam school closed for lack of money and its children were sent to school in Doña Ana. The Shalam children, now older, began to rebel against their strict upbringing. By 1900, the colony was destitute and Shalam was abandoned. Andrew Howland sold the land for $60,000 in 1907--a desperate transaction considering that more than $300,000 had been invested in the property.

Although Newbrough's ideal society failed to survive, the railroad attracted many an entrepreneur whose talents thrived in the growing city. In 1886 the *Rio Grande Republican* reported that Albert Ellis "the colored Las Cruces barber, who saw and heard everything" opened a shop on Main Street, offering hot baths for 50 cents, haircuts for 35 cents and a shave for a quarter. Gee Lee's laundry advertised washing

RAIN

I remember rain upon leaves
on the streets I walked to work.
Rain has its own memory of cities
and holds the sound of each within
as a shell twists tight the sea.
Lift rain to your ear and you may hear
the streets still humming, alive
in Manhattan, Omaha, Athens, Albany.
Now, in the desert, I open
the window when it rains, invite in
the smell of sage and buffalo grass,
listen for the plunk of each drop
as it strikes the leaves and plays
the earth as an ancient harp,
wherever rain leaves its mark,
where sky meets sky over us.

Nancy Peters Hastings

and ironing services plus meals for 25 cents.

Because there were no banks between El Paso and Albuquerque, Numa Reymond offered his store's safe for deposits, which were nearly always in gold. In July 1883, a local landowner named A.H. Raynolds established the Doña Ana Bank of Las Cruces, but the next year sold out to Job M. Evans who improved the financial health of the ailing bank. Evans' principal distinction, however, is that he became the town's first bank embezzler, who upon his departure left the bank "in a highly muddled condition." The bank was then sold to Henry Bowman, his father and brother who also had loan, real estate and insurance businesses.

In addition to its role as a banking center, Las Cruces also served as the headquarters for federal and county governments. Within six months after the arrival of the railroad, the Doña Ana County seat and other key government offices were moved from Mesilla to Las Cruces. By 1883 the 3rd Judicial District Court and the U.S. Land Office also had left Mesilla for Las Cruces.

The era of economic prosperity in Las Cruces was accompanied by good times of another sort. The coming of the railroad increased the number of saloons where "every available room is being sought after and adorned with all kinds of bar fixtures." The local paper reported "eighteen saloons and five dance halls in full blast every night... ." The saloons, outfitted in Victorian excess, were important gathering places for the socially and politically powerful. Some saloons even boasted reading rooms.

Although Las Cruces had its share of lawlessness, it was never a Wild West town. For good reason. It was the only town in New Mexico to organize a police force in response to the coming of the railroad and the "hordes of desperate characters" that preceded its arrival. In January 1881 the town hired a four-man police force with James H. White as its police chief. By April the railroad crews were moving away from Las Cruces and the force was disbanded. But by fall the editor of the *Rio Grande Republican* was complaining about "the everlasting shooting on the streets at night," and recommended a few good whippings to solve the problem. Instead, the police force was reinstated.

After the railroad crews had passed through Las Cruces, the fretful editor seemed relieved when the prostitutes followed along. "The soiled doves, late of the now defunct Centennial dance hall," he reported, "are shaking the dust of Las Cruces and will take up their habitations in Silver City, El Paso and other towns of

the south." Indeed, Las Cruces seems to have been able to "export" most of its sinners to El Paso, which was busy cultivating its Wild West reputation, or other nearby communities that quietly tolerated less than wholesome activities.

However, Doña Ana County was not without its notoriety. And it came in the person of a 6'5" southerner named Patrick Floyd Jarvis Garrett. After the Civil War, Pat Garrett rode away from his family's ruined Louisiana plantation, drifting first to Texas where he took up buffalo hunting and then into New Mexico where he fought Indians. He was a crack shot and a dogged pursuer, just the qualifications New Mexico needed in a sheriff in 1880. His first duty was to bring in Billy the Kid for killing Sheriff Matthew Brady. The tenacious Garrett tracked the Kid down at Stinking Springs, capturing him on December 23.

A jury in Mesilla found the Kid guilty and Judge Warren Bristol ordered him transferred to Lincoln to be hanged for his crime. On April 28, 1881, the Kid bolted from the Lincoln

Main Street, *Las Cruces was where locals and travelers could find hotels, saloons, a barber shop, a bakery, and every kind of mercantile establishment where dry goods, groceries, clothes and shoes could be purchased. This photograph dating from about 1901 shows the busy thoroughfare looking south where the Loretto Academy sits at the end of the street nearly hidden by the dust.*

Lawmen *(l-r) Patrick F. Garrett, James R. Brent, and John W. Poe all sought the elusive Billy the Kid. Fifteen years after killing Billy, Garrett returned to Las Cruces from Texas to track down suspects in the Fountain murder case. Garrett was allegedly shot in the back of the head in 1908 by Wayne Brazel, who was later acquitted of Garrett's murder.*

courthouse, killing two deputys in the process. Once again, Garrett was in pursuit. At midnight on July 14, Garrett and the Kid encountered each other in a bedroom on Pete Maxwell's ranch, neither one sure of the other's identity in the dark. *"Quien es?"* the Kid asked, cocking his pistol. Without answering, Garrett fired, killing the Kid instantly with his first shot.

At first Garrett was considered "a glorious Godsend" for shooting the young outlaw. But as the Kid's legend grew, Garrett's fortunes waned. He went on to other ventures. And back to Texas. Then in 1896 Albert J. Fountain and his nine-year old son were reported missing, probably murdered, on the road to Las Cruces. Fountain, a prominent political and social leader in the Mesilla Valley, had been vigorously prosecuting cattle thieves in the Tularosa Basin when he disappeared. A wire went out to Garrett.

The town's political leaders promised him a deputy sheriff's salary of $300 a month to solve the Fountain murders. Garrett was soon on the trail of the three suspects, Oliver Lee, Bill McNew and Jim Gililland, tough cowboys from Texas who ran cattle of questionable ownership on Lee's Tularosa Basin ranch. He got McNew first. Garrett then went after the other two. After eight months in hiding and three years after Fountain's disappearance, Lee and Gililland finally surrendered to their friend and temporary deputy, Eugene Manlove Rhodes. By then, the case had turned into a celebrated political feud between Democrats who promoted the cowboys' innocence and Republicans who were just as sure of their guilt.

Albert Jennings Fountain *(left) moved to Mesilla in 1875 where he established a substantial law practice. He later defended Billy the Kid in the 1881 trial for the murder of Sheriff William Brady, for which Billy was found guilty. Fountain was also a colonel in the First Cavalry Regiment and led his militia column in search of Geronimo in 1885. The mystery of his death in 1896 still stirs questions of murder and motive today.*

Elder statesman *Oliver Lee (right) is pictured here in 1925 when he was the Republican floor leader in the New Mexico House of Representatives. "I have no doubt that the coat concealed a pistol," said S. Omar Barker, a friend and fellow House member. Barker believed that Lee thought enemies from long ago might try to even old scores. Lee had been charged with the 1896 murder of Albert J. Fountain. With Albert B. Fall as his defense attorney, Lee was found innocent at the conclusion of a notorious trial at Hillsboro.*

***Eugene Manlove Rhodes** escorted his friends Oliver Lee and Jim Gililland, both suspects in the murder of Albert J. Fountain, on the train to Las Cruces. Rhodes, a beloved writer of cowboy literature, wrote numerous works, which include 12 books, 60 short stories, and more than 30 poems. He is pictured here in 1913.*

Albert Bacon Fall, an ambitious Democrat, represented the cowboys, while Thomas Catron, a Republican and leader of the Santa Fe Ring (a politically and economically powerful group involved in land grant manipulations and business monopolies), spoke for the prosecution. The trial, held among a partisan, boisterous crowd, lasted 18 days. The jury took eight minutes to find the men not guilty. Lee then went back to ranching and on to the state legislature.

Garrett became a U.S. deputy marshall and continued to live in Las Cruces, chasing bank robbers and other desperados. For a time he served as customs collector in El Paso then in 1906 he returned to his ranch near Las Cruces, indebted to nearly everyone from Gov. George Curry to W.W. Cox, his neighbor to the south.

On Feb. 29, 1908, while on his way from his ranch to Las Cruces, Garrett was shot in the back of the head, killed instantly. His killer, one of Cox's cowboys named Wayne Brazel, pleaded self-defense. He and Garrett had a running argument over the fact that Brazel was grazing goats on land leased from Garrett and Garrett hated goats. The jury found young Brazel not guilty. That night, Cox held a barbecue at his San Augustine ranch to celebrate Brazel's acquittal.

When Garrett was killed Pres. Theodore Roosevelt remarked that Pat Garrett didn't just uphold the law in New Mexico, he introduced it. (Today, commuters on their way to White Sands sweep past the spot where Garrett was murdered, vaguely aware of the old lawman's role in bringing law and order to New Mexico.)

Before long, the process from lawlessness to law and order took a natural leap into politics. In fact, nearly everything that happened in Las Cruces during the three decades after 1880 involved politics. During that period several other counties had been carved out of Doña Ana County's immense territory, shrinking it to nearly one-tenth its original size. The reduction in effect, increased the political importance of Las Cruces, its largest city.

Here, politicians came in two types, Republicans, mostly Hispanics, who practiced politics with religious zeal, and Democrats who were mostly Anglos eager for a foothold in the new territory. At stake was the chance to control land and water, and to grab the power that would come with statehood.

The best way to ensure political victory was to bring in the votes. It was not uncommon for both parties to round up voters on election eve, prime them with whiskey, put them in a corral for safekeeping, and march them to the polls the next morning. Such practices led one editor to complain that "the money spent for whiskey and votes by the politicians of Las Cruces in the late election would have built an adequate system of water works . . . put the streets in decent condition and planted rows of trees along every important street."

Two different but equally remarkable men defined the politics of this era. Albert J. Fountain was a Yankee of ambiguous origins who came to the Mesilla Valley with the California Column in the 1860s. The young lieutenant found the valley much to his liking and in 1862 he married the young daughter of a prominent Hispanic family and settled down to practice law. By the 1880s Fountain had become the champion of the Spanish speaking community. With equal success he earned a legion of enemies in his vigorous prosecution of land grabbers and rustlers.

He founded the *Mesilla Independent,* using his forum as editor to promote his opinions on the issues of the day. He was a public spirited citizen who loved to organize parades and make speeches in both English and Spanish. And in 1888 at the invitation of the Republicans, he ran for the Territorial Legislature against a relative newcomer by the name of Albert Bacon Fall.

Fall was a southerner who had gone to Zacatecas, Mexico, to strike it rich in the mines but left only with a good command of Spanish. From there he went prospecting in Kingston, New Mexico, where he soon decided to give up mining in favor of more lucrative pursuits in Las Cruces. Besides, Fall had a pretty wife back in Texas whose poor health would benefit from southern New Mexico's dry, sunny climate.

In Las Cruces Fall opened up a real estate office and studied law, determined to make a place for himself in the territory. With that in mind, he ran for the Territorial Legislature, only to lose to Fountain. By then Fall had been admitted to the bar and began defending cases involving land titles, and water and mineral rights. Cattle rustling cases were his specialty. He once said he had defended 500 people accused of rustling and never lost a case. Fall soon found himself opposing Fountain in the courtroom as well in politics.

As their feud grew, Las Cruces began to take sides. Fountain's Republicans kept to the west side of Main Street, claiming the Palmilla Club (a first class saloon) and Numa Reymond's store as their territory. Fall's Democrats frequented Albert Ellis's barber shop and a few bars of their own. Outside the courtroom, Fall and Fountain avoided each other. One night, however, Ben Williams, one of

William W. Cox, *a prominent New Mexico cattle grower, owned the San Augustine Ranch on the east side of the Organ Mountains. After he died in 1923, the ranch was inherited by his son A.B. Cox, and became known as the Cox Ranch. Today, much of this property, which includes Dripping Springs and La Cueva, is part of the 30,000-acre Organ Mountain Recreation Area .*

Fountain's men, was walking home along Main Street when he found himself face-to-face with Fall and his brother-in-law Joe Morgan. They all started shooting at once. In the calamity, Williams and Morgan were slightly wounded. Fall and Morgan were arrested, but it was Williams and Fountain who were indicted--Fountain for allegedly hiring Williams to kill Fall. The judge threw the case out.

Eventually Fall beat Fountain for his seat in the legislature, then went on to serve both houses, and as associate justice of the New Mexico Supreme Court and territorial attorney general. When statehood came in 1912, Fall and his old nemesis Tom Catron were New Mexico's first senators. Later the Teapot Dome Scandal would give Fall the unhappy distinction of being the first cabinet officer convicted of a felony committed while in office.

The Third Judicial District Court *posed for their portrait in 1891. They are (l-r, front row) Judge Simon B. Newcomb, district attorney; Col. A.J. Fountain, assistant United States attorney; Judge John R. McFie, district judge; and A.L. Christy, district clerk. In the back row are (l-r) F.A. Kuns, deputy district clerk; Herbert B. Holt, official court reporter; and William E. Martin, court interpreter.*

With Fountain's mysterious death, and Fall's eventual departure, politics in Las Cruces settled down. By the turn of the century, Las Cruces had all the requirements of a civilized town. Meeting the evening train had become a popular pastime, while formal activities included a "Grand Phantom Ball" held at the home of Nestor Armijo. Beatrice Armijo masqueraded as a "Chinese lady of rank," Annie Cuniffe came as the "Goddess of Liberty," and John H. Riley fooled everyone with his disguise as a "Young Lady," according to the *Rio Grande Republican.* At less grand but equally popular Calico balls, ladies dressed in pretty prints brought matching fabric swatches to place in a basket. Each gentlemen drew one of these calico chances and then danced with the young lady whose dress matched the fabric.

In 1885 Las Crucens had contributed $150 toward organizing a community band, complete with a bass, cornet, piano and four violins. That year also saw the formation of the Las Cruces Dramatic and Musical Club. Its first performance was a localized version of "Pocahontas," with Albert J. Fountain in a lead role. The play was such a success that the troupe was asked to perform in El Paso and Albuquerque.

Also in 1885 Las Crucens were struck by "roller mania," flocking to Van Patten's Hall, which served as a skating rink, a 1,200-seat auditorium and fair exhibit building. In 1887 the Southern New Mexico Fair Association was formed, holding its first fair the next year. Activities included commercial displays, baseball and cowboy tournaments, a grand ball and performances by the Fort Bliss military band. However, by 1889 fair organizers had exhausted themselves and their funds. They decided instead to promote the community and its agricultural products through an exhibition car that would travel by rail to fairs in the east.

Baseball had become the "rage of the territory." The first organized game was played in June 1884 when a team from Organ defeated Las Cruces 41 to 12. A July 4 rematch was played at Organ in 108-degree heat where the "Organ Nine" again defeated Las Cruces. When the

St. Genevieve's Band *(below) "elicited much praise from the visitors from neighboring towns," said the* Rio Grande Republican. *The band, "one of which any western town would be proud," performed open-air concerts on summer evenings in the 1890s, which drew almost the entire Las Cruces population.*

The Dramatic Club's *(left) local operatic performance of* David, The Shepherd Boy *was billed as "El Grand Success" by the* New Mexico Collegian *in 1901. The cast of "pleasing and well trained voices" included Alfred Holt as one of Abigail's attendants, Roy R. Larkin as King Saul, Helen MacGregor as King Saul's daughter, Charles Post as one of Abigail's attendants, and Professor E.O. Wooten as David.*

***The 1896 tennis season** began early on the morning of February 8th. "Although it was rather cold before sunrise, Cruces players were on their courts practicing by the time it was light enough to see the ball," reported the* New Mexico Collegian. *Despite their early efforts, Las Cruces fell to the favor of the college team in the last game. Members of the teams include (l-r, front row) C.W. Ward, Katherine Stoes, Alice Branigan, Mr. Stevens, and Jack Fountain; (middle row) Edith Dawson, Fannie Blakesley, Miss Granger, and Millicent Barker; (back row) Dr. Wooten, Dr. Jordan, Miss Freeman, H.B. Holt, Miss Meade, Mr. Freeman, and F.C. Barker.*

game was over, both sides celebrated with a "vigorous attack on the prize--a barrel of beer," according to the *Rio Grande Republican.*

The women who came to Las Cruces during this period brought with them ideas for improving life in the frontier town. In 1894 a group of these women formed the Women's Improvement Association and set out to live up to their name. They first solicited funds to buy a hearse to replace the wooden wagon the town had been using in funeral processions. Next they bought a sprinkler wagon for the town's dusty streets. And since the children had no place to play but the streets, the group decided Las Cruces needed a park. Their persuasive efforts caused one man to remark that "the ladies . . . are always needing money for something and when they get the money . . . they start wanting money for something else." They got their park, then a library. (Today, the Women's Improvement Association operates from its own clubhouse across from Pioneer Women's Park.)

Almost from its inception, Las Cruces had acquired one of the most important symbols of a civilized town--a church. By 1877, the beloved St. Genevieve's, which had been built in 1859, had been transformed from a church of native adobe to a French-styled brick cathedral.

Although the Catholic church continued its dominant influence in Las Cruces, the railroad soon opened the territory to other denominations, leading one bishop to complain that the biblical societies of New England were sending "bands of missionaries, loaded with gold and astounding promises" to lure away Catholics. The circuit riding preachers hardly fit this description, but their influence was undeniable. The Episcopalians and Methodists had formed congregations in Las Cruces in the 1870s; the Presbyterians built their church in 1883, and the Baptists theirs in 1899. Most of the early Jewish settlers attended holy day services at El Paso's Mount Sinai Temple, which had been built in 1899.

Until 1880, the churches, Catholic and Protestant alike,

were the only educational institutions in Las Cruces. The Sisters of Loretto had arrived here a decade earlier to establish the Academy of the Visitation, a girls school offering an array of classes including orthography, reading, algebra, modern and ancient geography, lace work, and piano. The academy admitted children of all denominations for $200 a year in tuition and board. Because the cost excluded all but the children of the affluent, the academy also offered children from poor families free tuition.

When the push for public schools began in earnest in the 1880s, the move was bitterly opposed by the Catholic clergy, who had established the first widespread network of schools in the territory. Harry Newman, the publisher of the Las Cruces newspaper *Thirty-four,* was solidly behind the drive for a school, making generous use of the paper as his pulpit. He had as his opponent the Rev. Andres Eschallier, the Las Cruces parish

St. Genevieve's *Catholic Church was located on Main Street, on property that is now the Downtown Mall area. The church was constructed on the site of an existing small adobe church, which was built in 1859. St. Genevieve's is pictured here as it appeared around the turn of the century.*

priest who used *his* pulpit to preach in opposition. Rev. Eschallier said that public schools were "destructive of good morals," and referred to Newman's newspaper as a "contemptible sheet."

The editor eventually moved to El Paso and when District Attorney Simon B. Newcomb spearheaded the drive to create the Las Cruces School Association in January 1880, St. Genevieve's Father Pedro Lassaigne graciously supported the effort. By September a two-room adobe school was completed and furnished with the association's $1,200 budget. However, financial troubles plagued the little school and it was finally closed. By 1887 non-Catholic education in Las Cruces consisted of only "a little school conducted on Church Street . . . by the good wife of a dissolute lawyer," recalled Judge R.L. Young who was instrumental in founding the Las Cruces College.

Pioneer educator
Hiram Hadley opened Las Cruces College in 1888 in a two-room adobe building leased from Numa Reymond. Hadley, the "Father of Education in New Mexico" was a driving force behind the establishment of what is known today as New Mexico State University. Hadley remained a respected and valuable citizen of Las Cruces until his death in 1922.

That summer Hiram Hadley arrived in Las Cruces and before the year was out, interest in a private school had been replaced by a drive for an agricultural college. Hadley, a Quaker from Ohio, actually had come to Las Cruces to be near his ailing son and to invest in real estate. But when the town fathers learned of his educational background (he had established Hadley's Normal Academy in Indiana), they approached him with their plans for a college. Once organized, the group sold stock in their educational enterprise. Financed with $750 from the sale of these stocks, the two-room adobe college opened its doors Sept. 15, 1888 with 64 pupils and a tuition of $40 a year. The "college" filled all of the gaps in the Las Cruces educational system, serving as an elementary, college preparatory and business school all wrapped up in one.

The founders of the Las Cruces College, however, had their sights on a much bigger prize. Congress in 1862 and 1877 had provided for the establishment of at least one land-grant college in each state and authorized agricultural experiment stations at these colleges. The trustees (Hadley called them a "band of trained politicians") convinced the New Mexico Legislature in 1889 to establish New Mexico's land grant college and experiment station at Las Cruces.

On June 1, 1894, Hadley presented diplomas to the terri-

***Hiram Hadley** stands in front of the original building where Las Cruces College began. Enrollment for the first year of classes in 1888 was an encouraging 64 students, with tuition at $40 a year. The name was changed to the New Mexico College of Agriculture and Mechanic Arts in 1890 to reflect its status as a land grant college.*

***Classes** of the New Mexico College of Agriculture and Mechanic Arts began in McFie Hall, built in 1891, the first permanent construction on campus. The building became known as "Old Main" and housed the administrator, faculty offices, classrooms, a reading room, and the library. On Sept. 12, 1910, not long after the library had been moved, "Old Main" was destroyed by fire.*

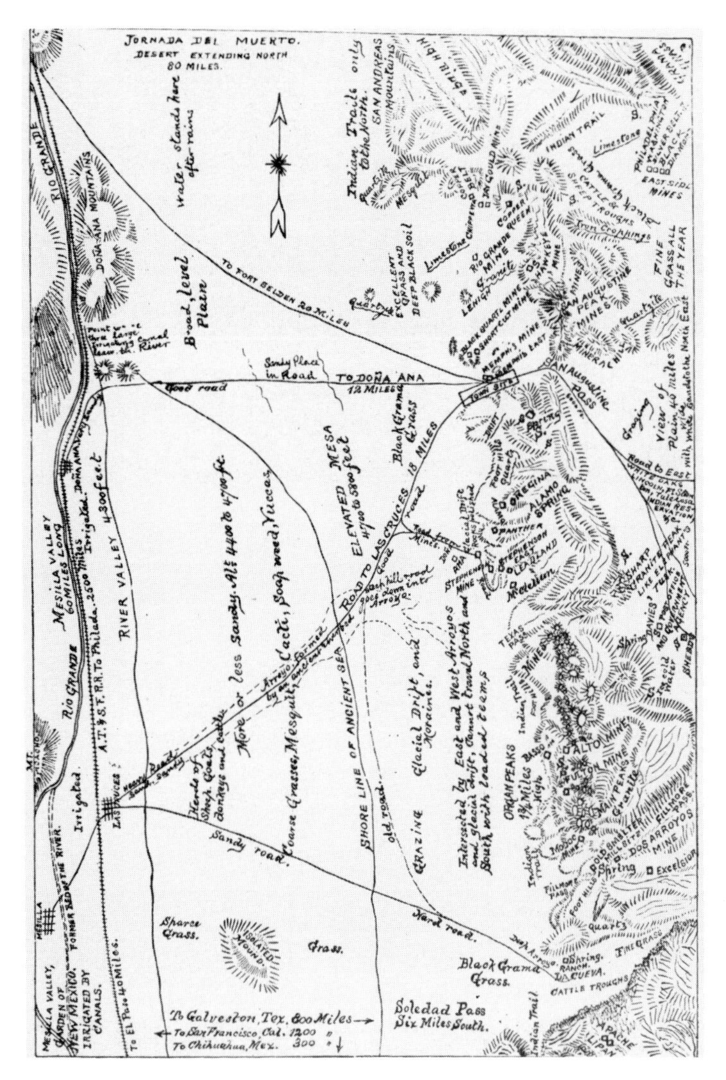

***The Organ Mountain** mining district was rich in copper, lead, silver and just enough gold to keep prospectors searching for the "mother lode." This map, which was printed on the back of a mining claim location notice, shows the location of several mines that existed in the Organs during the 1880s.*

tory's first college graduates, two women and three men. The *Rio Grande Republican* reported that commencement included "talented orators" and entertainment by the El Paso Orchestra, which had been hired for the occasion at "considerable expense."

The whirl of activity in Las Cruces during the last two decades of the century was fueled in part by the resurgence of an old industry--mining. In the 1880s politician and entrepreneur William Rynerson had expanded his business ventures to include mining. His Modoc Mine was producing lead and silver, and miners were taking thousands of tons of copper ore from the Torpedo Mine.

Merchants in both Las Cruces and the mining town of Organ 15 miles to the east cashed in on the boom. Twice a week, Henry Lesinsky operated a stage between his store in Las Cruces and Shedd's ranch in the Organs. For some $40, a prospector could buy a complete prospecting outfit, including "the patient and indispensable burro" and provisions for 40 days.

It was turquoise skies, not gold that lured the next wave of immigrants to New Mexico--health seekers. In the mid-1880s European doctors had developed the theory that clean, fresh air, particularly above 5,000 feet would cure tuberculosis. New Mexico's qualifications for providing "altitude therapy" were underscored when the federal government chose Fort Bayard and Fort Stanton as sites for the country's first federal tuberculosis treatment centers.

Las Cruces also provided ample accommodations for the health seeker. Eugene Van Patten's camp at Dripping Springs Canyon in the Organ Mountains was an ideal health retreat. In 1897 it became the first sanatorium in southern New Mexico. By 1906 the health spa included a 32-room hotel, complete with shaded verandas, green lawns and a bandstand.

In general, Las Cruces welcomed the "lunger invasion," which was at its peak from the 1880s until the 1920s. Most of the health seekers who could afford to relocate to New Mexico were well-educated young men who often stayed on to take up careers in the area. Las Cruces also benefitted from the influx of physicians who came to treat tubercular patients. Dr. Robert E. McBride, who came to Las Cruces in 1904 for his wife's health, established a sanatorium in town and then went on to build a successful general practice here.

New treatments, including drug therapy, eliminated the need for expensive "altitude cures" and finally ended the health seeker era in New Mexico by World War II. (Today, Van Patten's old resort at Dripping Springs attracts only hikers.)

As Las Cruces entered the twentieth century, a little breathless from the bustle of its past two decades, it faced yet another change. The river was being dried up. Everyone from farmers to ranchers to miners had tapped into the river from Colorado to Mexico. Since 1880, every piece of farmland in the Rio Grande Valley had been under irrigation and people had begun to complain of water shortages. During 1889 the Rio Grande was dry

***The Stephenson-Bennett** Consolidated Mining Company (above), pictured here about 1905, operated a mill in the Organ Mountains. The mill had an optimal output of up to 50 tons of ore a day. When silver and lead ore were first mined from the area in the early 1850s, it was carried out on men's backs and then crushed between large stones. Then burros hauled the ore to be smelted in an adobe furnace near Fort Fillmore some 16 miles away.*

***Many mines** (below) operated in the Organ Mountains throughout the turn of the century. These mine workers probably extracted several hundred tons of high-grade silver and lead ore from this shaft near Dripping Springs.*

__Van Patten's Camp__ was built by Col. Eugene Van Patten near Dripping Springs in the Organ Mountains during the late 1870s. The bank foreclosed on the once popular retreat and health resort around 1915.

from July until late fall, preventing farmers from irrigating nearly two-thirds of their farmland.

Although farmers in the Las Cruces area continued to produce good crops of alfalfa as well as grapes, figs and other fruits, drought was a continuing problem. By the summer of 1902 the river bed in the southern part of the valley was so dry that people began using it as a road. In September the college agricultural experiment station reported on the progress of studies to find more efficient methods for irrigating alfalfa under varying drought conditions.

While the farmers didn't realize it then, 1902 would be a turning point for them. The 1902 Reclamation Act authorized the U.S. Bureau of Reclamation to begin construction of dams on rivers throughout the West, including the Rio Grande. The reclamation service soon would begin looking for a site.

The state's aridity, it turned out, also was a factor in its 1902 losing bid for statehood. That objection was one in a long line of "differences" that kept New Mexico a territory longer than any other state. The languages and religions of its Indian and Spanish heritage, and indeed its arid climate were alien to easterners, who cast the votes. New Mexicans also were partly to blame for their nearly lost cause. They protested that statehood would bring taxes they couldn't pay, public schools they didn't want, and "land grabbers" they didn't need. Finally, politicians were for statehood if their party was in office at the time, but against it if their party was out of power and would not have had access to the political appointments that surely would come with statehood.

In 1902 New Mexicans had pinned their statehood hopes on Theodore Roosevelt. Before his election he had promised his New Mexico Rough Riders that "if New Mexico wants to be a state, you can count me in, and I will go back to Washington to speak for you or do anything you wish." However, Roosevelt's pre-election promises soon faded and statehood again was defeated.

By the time President Taft visited New Mexico in 1910, Albert J. Fall was fed up with campaign rhetoric. At a dinner honoring the president, Fall gave the key address taking the president to task for broken promises. Fall told the gathering that "the territory had a right to statehood and that presidents had a habit of making promises while touring the country, only to forget them later on." The crowd gasped at Fall's insolence, but Taft, who had not planned to make a speech, replied, "Judge Fall, I have heard your argument and am for your cause in spite of it."

On Jan. 6, 1912, Taft signed the proclamation admitting New Mexico into the Union. Turning to a witness, he said, "Well, it is all over. I am glad to give you life. I hope you will be healthy."

__A U.S. Post Office__ was opened in Las Cruces in 1854, the same year the Gadsden Purchase established the boundary between the United States and New Mexico. This photograph of the post office interior was taken in 1912, the year New Mexico attained statehood. Pictured here (l-r) are Capt. Thomas Branigan (the last Territorial post master in Las Cruces), Dave Chauvin, Mrs. Branigan, Wilson Wade, Johnny Lerma, and Fred Lemon.

Statehood, Water and War

1912 - 1945

Chile and pecans, *(previous pages) shown here against the familiar backdrop of the Organ Mountains, are two of the valley's most popular exports. Doña Ana County is the top ranked agricultural producer in the state.*

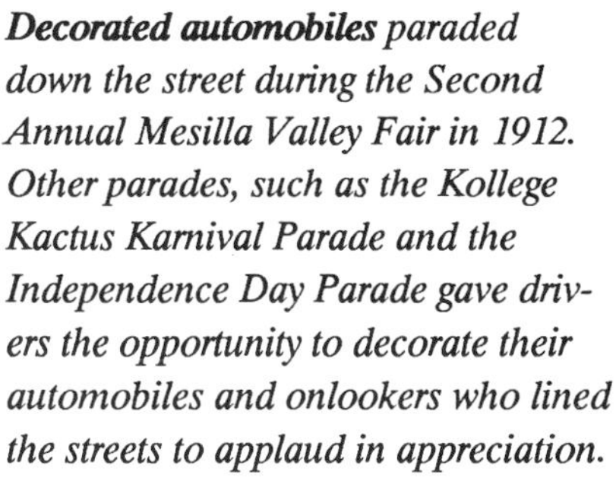

Decorated automobiles *paraded down the street during the Second Annual Mesilla Valley Fair in 1912. Other parades, such as the Kollege Kactus Karnival Parade and the Independence Day Parade gave drivers the opportunity to decorate their automobiles and onlookers who lined the streets to applaud in appreciation.*

In controlling the water,
the [Rio Grande Dam & Irrigation] Company will,
to a great extent, control the irrigable lands.

Dr. Nathan Boyd, 1895

On the morning of statehood, New Mexico woke to find itself part of a nation aspiring to global power. By then the United States had fulfilled its Manifest Destiny, won a couple of small wars, and nearly completed the Panama Canal. Europe, which had been uncommonly quiet for four decades, now rumbled with unrest.

The United States, like virtually every western nation, was feeling the social side effects of industrialization. Meanwhile, millions of immigrants flooded the country seeking opportunity and redefining the national character. Americans hosted the World's Fair in St. Louis, drove Model Ts and flocked to the movies. Women raised hemlines to their ankles and higher as they took up driving and other "modern" pursuits. Scientific discoveries during the century's first two decades marked the birth of a technological age that would prove both astounding and horrifying by the end of century. Within one generation Albert Einstein had formulated his Theory of Relativity, Orville and Wilber Wright had taken flight at Kitty Hawk, and Robert Goddard had sent a rocket into the atmosphere.

The age of discovery also saw the death of an old industry in the valley. By 1912, the mining boom in the Organ Mountains was over. Although a chemistry professor named A. Goss had managed to reap $1,023 in gold from a mine he leased during his 1902 summer vacation, speculators buying and selling claims now made more money than prospectors.

Although the boom was dead, the legend of the Lost Padre

Mine received another incarnation in 1937 when a sometime foot doctor named Milton Noss claimed he found gold bars stacked inside a cave at Victorio Peak. The cavern, "Doc" Noss said, also contained rooms full of church robes, religious figures, and silver and gold goblets. But in trying to enlarge the cave opening, he accidentally sealed the entrance, and like the legendary padre, was murdered before he could reveal its location. Today, a Noss grandson continues to search the Organs for the hidden mine.

By 1912 Las Cruces had taken on the look of small town America. Newer neighborhoods bore streets named for early citizens such as Lucero, Bowman, Van Patten and Griggs. While most of the city's nearly 4,000 residents still lived in adobe homes, more recent arrivals built houses reminiscent of St. Louis and San Diego. Builders abandoned adobe for conventional brick, fulfilling the 1880 prediction of the *Silver City Enterprise* that ". . . one thing is for certain, the day of the adobe is done in Las Cruces."

Main Street had become a mix of one-story plastered adobes, wooden store fronts, and brick two-story buildings. Telegraph poles paralleled the seven-block street, which was home to

__Automobiles__ had all but replaced horses on Las Cruces' Main Street by 1912. A variety of models were parked along the yet unpaved thoroughfare where a few years before had been the domain of the horse and buggy.

The college *(left) in 1914 offered a one-year course in automobile and gas engine repair. The college newspaper,* The Round Up, *reported that "the work is as near practical as possible" and "a great deal of instruction is given to the student taking this course in driving an auto."*

nearly every business in town. By 1915 complaints of a hitching post shortage along Main Street went unremedied as the automobile took up more and more parking places. The automobile had become so popular that the college instituted an automotive mechanics course to meet the "emergent needs" and President George Ladd drove to Roswell in his $1,600 Buick/Six to promote the new offering. Miss Christopherson, the high school domestic science teacher, told the student newspaper that "motoring" was her favorite pastime and travel her highest ambition. Motor trips to check the progress of the new dam were popular among city leaders and their wives.

However, the activities of family, church and community still kept most people close to home. In the spring of 1915 Elizabeth Garrett entertained the students and teachers at Central School by singing her compositions "The Mesilla Valley" and

Wednesday Literary Club *members (above) were creatively costumed for Character Day in 1911. Ordinarily, "the club does not serve refreshments other than for the mind," reported the* Rio Grande Republican, *"thus each meeting proves a feast of reason." However, on this "very unique and enjoyable occasion" an elaborate luncheon was served. The women are (l-r, front row) Mrs. Sexton, Mrs. Frenger, Mrs. Sutherland, Mrs. Stoes, and Miss French; (back row) Mrs. Llewellyn, Miss Daniels, Mrs. Monty, Miss Hill, Mrs. Broaddus, Mrs. Foster, and Mrs. Gerber.*

***Elizabeth Garrett,** daughter of Sheriff Pat Garrett, was the inspiring singer and composer who wrote the official state song, "O Fair New Mexico." "My father tried to bring peace and harmony to our country with guns," she said, "I would like to do my part with my music." She was photographed here with Tenne, her Seeing Eye dog.*

"New Mexico." The state legislature later adopted her "O Fair New Mexico" as the state song. Although she was blind, Pat Garrett's independent daughter traveled nationwide in her long career as a pianist and accomplished soprano.

That fall, the Southern New Mexico State Fair featured Mexican artisans and the Sixth Infantry Band from El Paso. Guided by the motto: "I'll do my little best," women were encouraged to enter the fair's ladies' department competition.

Las Cruces also hosted a tennis tournament in which more than 40 local players competed against players from El Paso, Roswell and other surrounding towns. The tournament promised to "place Las Cruces in the front rank of southwestern sporting towns." For the less athletic, the Star Theatre offered the film

"The Battle Cry of Peace" for a pricey 50 cents admission.

As Las Cruces took its place in the 20th century, the few traces of its Indian past were being preserved by a people of mixed Indian and Spanish heritage who joined together in Las Cruces to maintain their Indian identity. These were the descendants of the Indian and Spanish refugees who had settled in the missions at El Paso in the wake of the Pueblo Revolt. Two settlements inhabited by Piro and Manso Indians were attached to the Guadalupe Mission. After an epidemic in 1748, the surviving members of the two groups merged under a single tribal government. By the 1760s, as a result of intermarriage with other tribes at the mission, the Manso had lost their identity as a separate tribe.

With the El Paso settlements continuing to decline, Manso descendants from the Guadalupe

Los Danzantes *have danced in front of the church in Tortugas every year since 1914 in celebration of their heritage. Each December 10-12 the people of Tortugas honor Nuestra Señora de Guadalupe with a fiesta. Ceremonies include a procession with the image of Our Lady of Guadalupe, dances from various groups, a climb up Tortugas Mountain, prayer, and traditional food. This group is pictured here in about 1930.*

Mission, along with others from neighboring missions and nearby Indian pueblos formed a community in Las Cruces. In 1885 the *Rio Grande Republican* reported that they performed their traditional Guadalupe Day dances before St. Genevieve's Catholic Church.

***Cantaloupes** of the finest quality were a highly productive and profitable crop in the Mesilla Valley in the early 1900s. Some Mesilla Valley farmers who depended entirely on the local market, realized a net profit of $420 per acre. Fruits and vegetables were the favored crops before the dam was built.*

Theirs was the "Indian chorus" Bishop Henry Granjon saw performing with "drums, hums, jumps and dances" in front of St. Genevieve's during his visit in 1902. In 1910 after failing to complete their chapel in Las Cruces, the group moved its ceremonies to Tortugas, a small village just south of Las Cruces. The parishioners built a Catholic chapel there in 1914.

Since then, the Fiesta of Our Lady of Guadalupe has been held in the village each year from December 10-12. The three-day fiesta, part religious ceremony and part homecoming celebration, includes candlelight processions, dances, prayers and feasting. On December 11, participants make the four-mile pilgrimage to the top of Tortugas Mountain where they celebrate Mass. While still daylight, the women and children descend the mountain. Then just past sundown, the men start down, their paths lighted by small fires that can be seen from all over the Mesilla Valley.

The newspaper's commanding motto, "Boost for New Mexico or Get Out," reflected the mood of a self-assured community in the summer of 1915. Within the year Elephant Butte Dam would be completed and would bring certain prosperity. So said the paper. And the land promoters. And even the farmers.

The dam had been a long time in coming. In 1888 the El Paso City Council on the advice of Col. Anson Mills, an army engineer, decided to build an international dam three miles above El Paso at the United States/Mexican border. There, half the flow of the Rio Grande would be diverted to Mexico and half to the United States. Colonel Mills said the proposed dam would solve El Paso's flooding and drought problems, and resolve Mexico's claims against the United States for causing water shortages in the Juárez Valley. Fortunately for the Mesilla Valley, Washington failed to approve El Paso's plan. The dam at El Paso would have created a lake 15 miles long and seven miles wide, destroying 40,000 acres of Mesilla Valley farmland.

Before long, Las Cruces had its own proposal and Dr. Nathan Boyd to promote it. Boyd's Rio Grande Dam and Irrigation Company recommended building a dam at Elephant Butte, about 125 miles north of El Paso. Under Boyd's plan, landowners would relinquish one-half their land to the company in return for water rights to the other half. And to receive the water, farmers would then pay a perpetual rent to the company. "In controlling the water," Boyd wrote, "the company will, to a great extent, control the irrigable lands." The plan promised to make rich men of them all. When his pitch failed to interest enough investors in the United States, he headed for England where he convinced British investors to put $1.6 million into the project. In 1895 the Secretary of the Interior approved construction of Elephant Butte Dam, with the stipulation that it be built within five years.

El Paso was furious. A dam at Elephant Butte would make

Construction *(above) on the dam at Elephant Butte finally began in 1911 after land acquisition difficulties had stalled earlier attempts. Persistent politicians and engineers helped make the dam a reality. The railroad was also crucial to the dam's creation as heavy equipment and supplies were transported by rail from the main line at Engle to the dam site nine miles away.*

Workers *(below) installed balanced valves at Elephant Butte Dam during construction in 1914. When the dam was completed in May 1916, it created the world's largest man-made reservoir.*

their dam useless and ruin their careful negotiations with Mexico. The El Paso proponents, citing an obscure law on tampering with a navigable river, received a court injunction halting construction at Elephant Butte. The case wound its way through the courts until May 3, 1903, when a judge ruled that the Rio Grande was not a navigable river. However, El Paso's stalling tactic succeeded in preventing Boyd's company from meeting its construction deadline and caused it to lose its right to build the dam. Once again, El Paso pushed for its international dam. Residents of the Mesilla Valley fumed that the plan for the dam was the "most nefarious and barefaced scheme of public robbery ever invented in the United States." In the end, the two factions succeeded only in killing each other off. And then the government stepped in.

John Hay, President Roosevelt's Secretary of State, decided that a dam at Elephant Butte would provide enough water for the Mesilla Valley and El Paso, as well as Mexico. Hay persuaded the newly established Bureau of Reclamation to undertake its construction. As soon as the way for the dam was clear, water users in the Mesilla Valley and El Paso put aside their differences and organized to finance their share of the project costs. Their lands fell under the Homestead Act, with each farmer obligated to repay his share of the construction costs in return for water rights. The cost of the entire project was estimated at $7.2 million, or $40 an acre on some 180,000 acres of land. By September Mesilla Valley farmers had pledged 125,518 acres to the government as security for repayment of construction costs.

The federal government tried to discourage speculators and encourage family-sized farms by limiting project farms to no more than 160 acres. Contrary to the government's intentions, promoters and speculators soon busied themselves buying and selling land. Prices for cultivated farmland that sold from $20 to $40 an acre in 1904, doubled by 1908 and rose to $125 an acre by 1915. The water users associations in El Paso and the Mesilla Valley even established an

***Farmers** gather at the Temple of Agriculture, the name H.H. Brook gave to the building housing Doña Ana County Farm Bureau and Elephant Butte Irrigation District offices. The farm bureau was established in 1917 and was a founding member of the New Mexico Farm Bureau.*

"Immigration Bureau" to publicize project lands. The more landowners, they reasoned, the more people to help pay off the water debt. Not to be outdone, the *Las Cruces Citizen* listed 20 groups (including jewelers, geologists, fishermen and prison reformers) that could find "health, happiness and prosperity" in the valley.

Land ownership also changed in response to the coming of the dam. Traditionally, Hispanic farmers in the valley had owned their farms outright and produced enough crops to sustain their families. But the combination of project debt and land profits induced many to sell their lands to newcomers, mostly Anglos who came to the valley between 1900 and 1920. The Anglos in turn sold to other hopefuls, who then sold to newer arrivals. By the time the dam was built, three-fourths of all Anglo-owned farmlands and half of those held by Hispanics had changed hands.

When it was completed in 1916, the dam was magnificent. Men and machines had created the world's largest manmade lake. Behind the dam Elephant Butte stood in the waters like a stranded beast who had given up and gone to sleep. Downstream, however, news of the dam's completion sent farmers to work clearing new lands for irrigation.

Their enthusiasm soon was replaced by new worries. Almost immediately, the valley became waterlogged. Most farmers, unaccustomed to an abundance of water, over-irrigated their crops. In addition, standing water and high evaporation rates left soils encrusted with alkali. By 1920, an additional $1.5 million spent on drains had solved most of the drainage problems. The cost of land leveling and leaching to alleviate the alkali problem ran as high as $50 an acre.

Economic survival meant farmers needed to change how they farmed and what they grew. One farmer recalled that they "went crazy with cotton," plowing under alfalfa and tearing out orchards and vineyards to plant the new cash crop. Cotton prices were so high in the mid-1920s that income from one acre of cotton equalled the value of the acre where it was grown. By the

__Cotton__ was first planted commercially in the Mesilla Valley in 1919 and quickly became the valley's major cash crop. Representatives of Doña Ana County's Cooperative Extension Service and the Farm Bureau were on hand to celebrate the season's first bale of the "white money maker."

end of the decade three-fourths of the valley's farmers made most of their income from cotton.

During this time, events beyond the valley also brought social change to Las Cruces. Residents energetically joined the national debate on the evils of tobacco and alcohol. Dr. McBride urged students to "boycott Dr. Alcohol" for the sake of strong bodies, while members of the Anti-Tobacco League threw violators into a horse trough. Front page editorials called the saloon "a constant menace to good order and good government." When Prohibition later became law, old-timers simply returned to drinking homemade wine, while bootleggers got their supply from Mexico. At night horses packing liquor in metal cans would cross into New Mexico from Mexico to a meadow between Santa Teresa and Sunland Park in southern Doña Ana County. There, bootleggers would transfer the cans to waiting Model Ts and then head north along the Reclamation road for Las Cruces and Albuquerque.

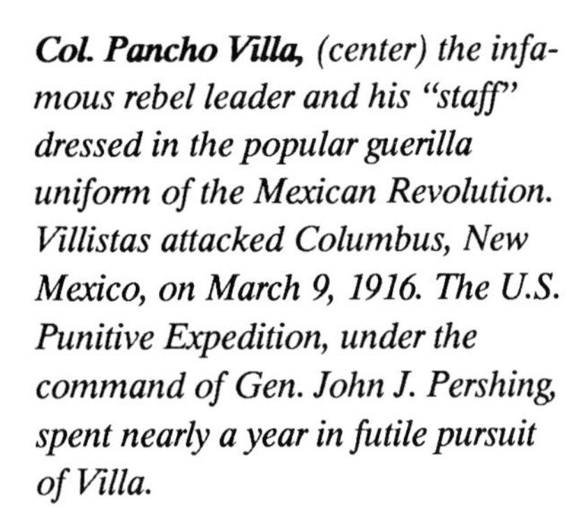

Col. Pancho Villa, *(center) the infamous rebel leader and his "staff" dressed in the popular guerilla uniform of the Mexican Revolution. Villistas attacked Columbus, New Mexico, on March 9, 1916. The U.S. Punitive Expedition, under the command of Gen. John J. Pershing, spent nearly a year in futile pursuit of Villa.*

The Mexican Revolution spilled over into the United States when Pancho Villa's troops raided Columbus, New Mexico, before dawn on March 9, 1916. Villistas torched and looted the town, killing 17 Americans. Although caught off guard, within twenty minutes the 350 U.S. soldiers stationed at Columbus were in quick pursuit of the Villistas heading toward Mexico. Within a week the United States named the Fort Bliss commanding general, John J. Pershing, as head of the Punitive Expedition into Mexico to capture Villa.

Less than 100 miles from the battle, Las Cruces waited jittery and alert, fearing Villa would strike again nearby. Automobiles, gas tanks filled, were at the ready for quick escape. The fact that New Mexico A & M graduate Charles D. Miller had been among the casualties brought the raid close to home. Some 30 college students were called to border duty.

By the time Pershing's troops were withdrawn nearly a year later (with Villa still at large), Las Cruces had settled down enough to enjoy its nearly ringside seat of the events. In one instance when a company of troops came through town, Father Vandermaessen entertained its officers at a noonday dinner. The Sisters of Loretto then invited the entire company to attend Benediction in the convent chapel, afterwards serving refreshments and presenting each of the visitors with a badge of the Sacred Heart. "The boys," it was reported, "responded by giving an impromptu musical entertainment to their hostesses."

The distractions of the Mexican Revolution were soon replaced with a more focused concerns when in April 1917 the United States entered World War I. In June, Las Cruces Mayor John May declared a municipal holiday so that all men between the ages of 21 and 30 could register for the nation's first draft. College enrollment reflected the war effort as females soon outnumbered males on campus, although enrollment later increased as soldiers entered the college under the Student Army Training Corps program. The demands of war were reflected in the 1918 graduating class, which had only seven graduates, mostly women.

Wartime insecurity gave rise to the conformity of "Americanism" and a fear and distrust of foreigners. Farmers in El Paso and Las Cruces worried over competition from "alien agriculturalists" who were renting large tracts of land in the valley. While a newspaper article by farmer W.T. Scoggins conceded that Japanese immigrants were "masters of the art of hoeing, transplanting and irrigating," he ended by asking, "Must red blooded American farmers who sent their sons to war, who bought Liberty Bonds, who built the dam and reclaimed the desert, turn over their livelihood to Orientals?" Sheriff Lucero warned all "enemy aliens that they were not allowed guns . . . wireless bombs . . . or codebooks." They could turn such items over to him, and with a receipt he promised they could reclaim them at the end of the war.

But in October 1918 the war and the "alien problem" took a

THE VOICES OF MY DESERT

Beginning this new trail, with the resonance
of shifting earth about me, I hear calls
distancing the crow voices of my childhood,

the wolf cry of my middle age. The sun
is an ancient symbol above me and God knows
what the mountains, spirit blue on the horizon

mean. Silence stands within me as without
desert stirs to its own subtle communication.
There is time, always, to wonder, doubt.

New Mexico is a myth, an ancient whirlpool
of time where moments stand still just before
being sucked down to other planes, other
hours.

We hold time back through rituals, dances
that stir the seconds like flecks of sand
beneath our feet, eternities of the possible.

I write down the words I hear, but I know
it is the Dead who speak them. Our ears
are tuned to the past, hear, hear the days

less clearly than the flute-songed nights
with their last owls whitefaced as moons
swooping low for the poisoned, dying mice.

The ghosts of wolves ring our hills.
Those birdcries, Comanche songs drifting
up for wartrails; the click of steel

in the night, prospectors or old soldiers
sharpening the edge of darkness to a keen
wind that blows all the stories away.

Keith Wilson

Students *(above) of Miss Lissie Etheridge's (far right, back row) third and fourth grade classes pose for their 1899-1900 school year picture in front of South Ward School. The school opened in 1893, the first public school in Las Cruces.*

Loretto Academy, *(left) pictured here in the 1930s, was built on 15 acres of land at the foot of Main Street that had been purchased by the Sisters of Loretto in 1870. Competition from other Catholic schools and a new Loretto Academy in El Paso finally closed the school in 1944. A shopping mall was built on the site in 1965.*

back seat to the Spanish influenza epidemic. Although many believed New Mexico's sunshine and its distance from big cities would protect them from the disease, more than a 1,000 New Mexicans died in the epidemic. The flu struck nearly every home in Las Cruces, and at the height of the outbreak in October and November both the college and the public schools were closed. Soldiers in the student barracks were hit particularly hard although not as badly as those stationed in the "rain soaked camps back in New England," according to one observer.

When the war was over, young men came back to a town eager to leave hardship behind and take up finer things. On summer nights, young audiences delighted to the Patio Players who performed skits and songs under the trees at St. Genevieve's. For the more sophisticated, the Las Cruces Orchestra played Beethoven and Bellini. Of one performance, a newspaper critic wrote, "If more of this type of concerts were given, the abominable curse 'jazz' would be a thing of the past."

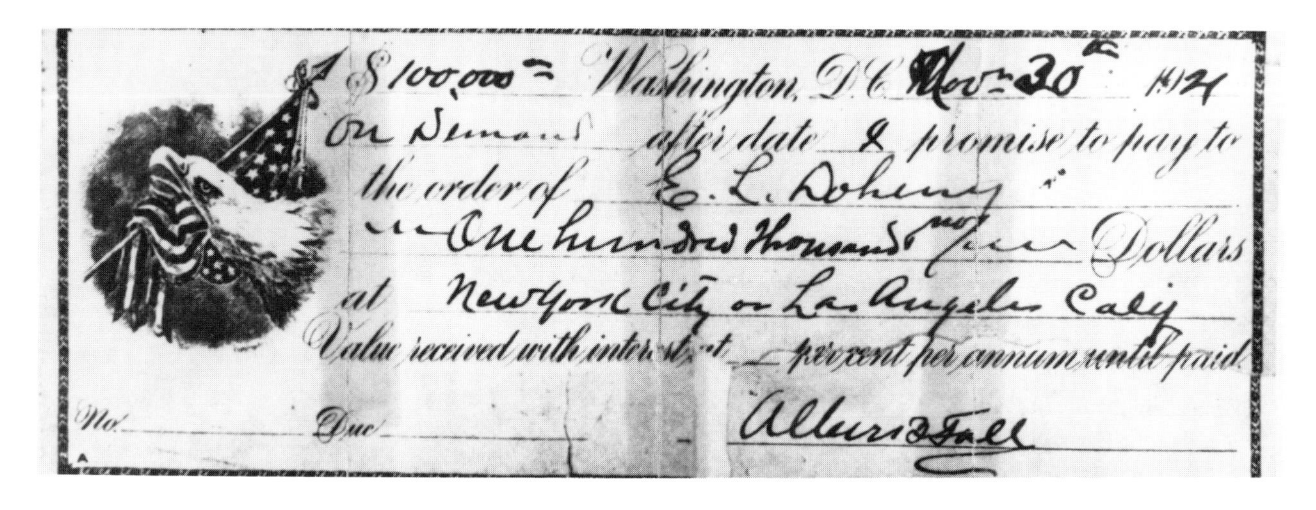

$100,000 = Washington, D.C. Nov-30th 1921
On Demand after date I promise to pay to
the order of E. L. Doheny
One hundred thousand no/100 Dollars
at New York City or Los Angeles Cali
Value received with interest at ___ per cent per annum until paid.
No. ___ Due ___
Albert B Fall

Evidence *such as this $100,000 check was used to convict Albert Bacon Fall of bribery charges in the Teapot Dome Scandal. Fall, then the U.S. Secretary of the Interior, explained the checks as legitimate loan payments to his old friend Edward L. Doheny. In 1931 Fall was sentenced to prison. Doheny, however, was acquitted of receiving any bribe in the scandal.*

During the 1920s New Mexico had finally begun making a conscious effort to improve its public education system. Although territorial legislatures as far back as 1860 had required public schools in all communities, they made no provision to finance them. Then in the 1870s several laws awarded income to the schools from fines levied for transgressions such as engaging in sports on Sunday and marrying "close relatives." Property, however, was not to be taxed to support schools. Finally in 1912 the state constitution established public lands as a source of income for schools. From then on, the state has provided the bulk of the total revenue for education.

It is believed that the first public school classes in Las Cruces were held in about 1893 in a two-room adobe building that previously had housed the Las Cruces College. Two years later, C.W. Ward was listed as principal of the school, which became known as the South Ward School. The building must have been enlarged by this time in order to accommodate the school's 279 pupils.

On July 9, 1904, Isidoro Armijo, Thomas Branigan and José Gonzales met to organize Doña Ana County School District No. 2. Armijo was elected chairman. They then hired five teachers, including Fannie French, at salaries ranging from $45 to $55 a month, and three janitors at $5 and $10 a month for the school term. Professor W.O. Evans was hired as principal for $80 a month.

By the next year, the ambitious board had contracted Trost and Trost Architects to design a new school, for which the firm was to be paid $286.50. Miss French moved to the new Central School and received a raise to $60 a month. By 1914 Central School had become the high school with Miss French as its principal. In 1925 the Union High School District was formed and ninth through twelfth grades were moved from Central to the new Union High School building on Alameda Boulevard.

In 1927 a new Catholic school, Holy Cross, was completed. The school had been built using donated labor and materials and financed partly from 25-cent admission fees to entertainment fundraisers. At the same time, the venerable Loretto Academy of the Visitation, which at its peak consisted of 40 rooms and a 3,000-volume library, was slowly losing students to the new Loretto Academy in El Paso. In 1944 the old school was sold to the Franciscan Fathers who converted it to a seminary.

Early in its history the Las Cruces school system was integrated, although a 1906 school board ruling prohibited children from speaking Spanish on the school grounds. Beginning in the 1920s, however, Southerners coming into the area pressured the school district to segregate. On the first day of the 1926 school term, black students were sent to school at Phillip's Chapel, which belonged to the African Church. Later, black students attended Booker T. Washington School on Solano Drive. In 1946 the Gadsden School District bussed black students from Vado to "the black school" in Las Cruces, some 25 miles away. Las Cruces schools remained segregated until 1954.

While the nation's rich got richer during the 1920s, they failed to notice that the poor also got poorer--so poor in fact that

The Rev. Hunter Lewis came to Mesilla Park in 1905 and served as a missionary of the Episcopal Church for 43 years. "Preacher" Lewis, as he was called by the students at the college, married Edith Weymouth in 1906. They are shown here with five of their six children. Reverend Lewis was known as the "knitting parson" because he knitted baby blankets and crocheted baby caps for the infants he baptized.

by 1929 workers could no longer afford the consumer goods that had fueled the economy in the first place. What farmers had known for nearly a decade, took Wall Street by surprise on October 24, 1929--the nation was broke.

As early as 1923 the First National Bank had quit making loans for land investments because Elephant Butte Dam had not brought the prosperity it expected. And in 1926, Mesilla Valley farmers saw the market fall for nearly all produce, as well as for their money-maker--cotton. Cotton prices nationally dropped from 29 cents a pound in 1923 to 6 1/2 cents in 1934, with some local farmers receiving as little as 4 cents a pound. Under the Agricultural Adjustment Act of 1933, the government, in hopes of raising prices, paid farmers not to plant cotton. In some years farmers received more money for not growing cotton than they would have for growing it.

It was during this shaky economic period, that W.J. Stahmann and his son Deane decided to take up farming in the valley. The Stahmanns were an innovative and adventurous family that had come to New Mexico by way of Texas from their home in Bruce, Wisconsin. W.J., in search of a healthier climate for his tubercular wife, in 1907 had loaded his family onto two barges and floated down the Mississippi River to Arkansas. From there they moved to Fabens, Texas, where he set up his honey making business. In a tradition his son would follow, Stahmann soon added to his enterprise, a tomato canning plant, a cotton gin, and a cotton compress.

Although W.J. died in 1929, Deane continued the Mesilla Valley farming operation, which by 1936 totaled 4,000 acres. At first Deane Stahmann grew field crops, including cotton, along with a variety of fruits and vegetables. That practice changed in 1932 when Deane found a bargain in pecan trees. The trees had been ordered by a farmer in El Paso who found himself unable to pay for the delivery. Deane, who had been looking for an alternative to cotton, bought the cut-rate trees and planted them on his farm.

While waiting for the trees to mature, he grew cotton among the rows and brought in geese to weed and fertilize the fields. After a visit to the Stahmann Farms in 1939, famed reporter Ernie Pyle wrote of Deane, "He intends to do his own processing and marketing. He will advertise, propagandize, beat the drums, and turn us into a nation of pecan eaters whether we like it or not." Undaunted by a depressed economy, Dean Stahmann forged ahead with his innovative approach to farming and marketing that one day would make Stahmann Farms the largest pecan orchard in the world.

"The lesson of hard times," William McSain told the State Farmers Convention in 1932, "shows that we got into debt during prosperous times and then paid off our debts in hard times." McSain, the First National Bank president, certainly knew what he was talking about. When a run started on the bank in September 1931, McSain closed its doors. Although he proclaimed the bank "absolutely solvent," and said it would reopen when "the hysteria subsides," the bank stayed closed for 55 days. Bankers also were faced with the dilemma of whether or not to foreclose on ranchers and farmers delinquent on their land loans, since the banks could not even find buyers for the properties they already owned from earlier foreclosures.

For most people in Las Cruces, however, the depression just meant more belt tightening in already lean times. Bank closings meant little to those with no money put into the bank. The despairing faces of those passing through town were sober reminders that life elsewhere could be much worse. Picacho Avenue earned the title "Little Oklahoma" when it became a trade route of sorts for the stream of destitute travelers on their way to California. (Today, second-hand stores still line the thoroughfare.)

The government, through a series of emergency unemployment relief programs, did its best to keep Las Cruces employed. Young men in the Civilian Conservation Corps were put to work at Elephant Butte Dam, while workers in town built three schools, including Court Junior High. Genevieve Lucero tells of working on the Doña Ana County Federal Sewing Project. She recalls working in a large room at the courthouse, along with several other women from around the county, sewing T-shirts and blue

***Women's Club members** proudly proclaim the 50th anniversary of the club in this 1944 parade. Officially established as the Women's Improvement Association, today the group continues its tradition of civic improvement nearly a century after its founding.*

jeans. In 1930 the college requested $600,000 from the government to pay for building construction, and workers in Las Cruces received more than $80,000 from the federal payroll for twelve weeks' work in 1934.

With the attack on Pearl Harbor on Dec. 7, 1941, the government quickly retooled into a war making machine. More than 25,000 troops were stationed at El Paso, whose population now numbered more than 100,000. Albuquerque, still in its high-tech infancy, counted a population of 35,000. And although Las Cruces in 1941 was still a small town of 8,000, it too would be transformed by the war.

In the fall of 1942 college enrollment fell 30 percent as students went off to war. In what one professor called a "relief program for universities," the government boosted college enrollment, which consisted mainly of women students, with 350 members of the Student Army Training Corps. Vacant CCC buildings were used as barracks for naval trainees and later to house prisoners of war.

Several units of the New Mexico National Guard were called up early in the war to serve in the Philippines. The War Department believed that these bilingual troops could adapt more readily to the hardships of the Philippines. When the Philippines fell to the Japanese, a disproportionate number of the American POWs were New Mexicans who endured forced marches to the death camps on Bataan. Before war's end, 124 of the college's former students had died serving in the military.

The war also rekindled old fears about foreigners buying up farmland. About 1,000 farmers in the valley signed pledges binding themselves not to sell land to "alien Japanese." Feelings against the Japanese were so intense that when the Emergency Farm Labor Program began using POW labor to ease the wartime labor shortage, Japanese POWs were not even considered. Although the Italian POWs made good company, they proved temperamentally unsuited for picking cotton. In contrast, German POWs, primarily from the Africa Corps, relished their work in the fields. They were paid the prevailing wage, of which all but 75 cents a day was held in the bank for them until war's end.

Many New Mexicans *served in the South Pacific during World War II. Pictured here in about 1942 are (l-r) Capt. James Baird, Capt. Otto Horton, Col. Hugh Milton II, Lt. John H. Campbell, Capt. Mansil Schrivner, and Capt. Mark Radoslovich.*

Navy pilot *Gerald W. Thomas served with Torpedo Squadron Four during his 41 months of active during World War II. Dr. Thomas was president of New Mexico State University from 1970-1984 and is currently a consultant in natural resource management and world food production.*

John Nakayama had been one of the foreign-born Orientals who bought land in the name of his American-born son. Nakayama, whose family had a 1200-year tradition of rice farming, had come from Japan in 1908 to the Mesilla Valley by way of Nebraska. There he worked cattle and farmed the high plains. He left Nebraska's cold winters behind and headed for Las Cruces where he had heard several Japanese families had settled. He first rented land in Doña Ana on what had been the Shalam Colony farm. His son Roy was born there in what had been the Children's House.

Hard work and a few years later, Nakayama owned 25 acres, then 105 acres, then leased a few hundred acres more. The five Nakayama children were involved, bright students as well as invaluable to the family farm. At the outbreak of World War II, Roy, the youngest, was attending New Mexico A & M.

But by the fall of 1944 Roy had been captured by the Germans during the Battle of the

Bulge. By the time the war was over he had spent seven months as a prisoner of war and weighed 87 pounds. When he returned home to finish college, however, he was refused admission because he was Japanese. His former professors challenged the decision and he was soon admitted, graduating in 1948. Later, professor Nakayama returned to the college with a Ph.D. where he taught horticulture and became a distinguished pecan and chile researcher.

During those war years, people still knew most everybody in town and conducted their business on Main Street. Wages were still low (work at the cotton compress paid 25 cents an hour), and most of the streets still were not paved. And just about everyone knew the government was conducting secret research in the Tularosa Valley near White Sands, some 40 miles east of Las Cruces.

In the early dawn of July 16, 1945, Raymundo Enriquez was already out in his fields irrigating. Then a few seconds past 5:30 "the sky opened up and everything became day," he remembered. The sky flashed a brilliant white, sound waves rumbled in the distance. Within seconds, the quiet darkness returned. Reymundo had no idea at the time, but he had just witnessed the explosion of the world's first atomic bomb. Within a month, the war would be over.

__Just prior to World War II,__ when this photograph was made, the Rio Grande Motor Company invited Las Crucens to "Motor in the modern way in the Chevrolet Master De Luxe." General Motors' first postwar sport sedan, the new "Stylemaster," made its debut in Las Cruces in 1945. The "Stylemaster" sounded "an appealing note in sleek modern styling." That same year, GM introduced the new, improved Hydro-Matic Drive, "which afforded fully automatic shifting without a clutch pedal."

The Las Cruces Community Theatre
317

Sunbelt City

1946 - Present

It is that place where, whenever you return to it,
your soul releases an inner sigh
of recognition and relaxation.

PATRICK SALE, *Return to Paradise*

With the homecoming parades over and the uniforms packed away, young veterans like Eduardo Fernandez took familiar paths to home and family. Although he left for war with a biology degree, farming now seemed a more profitable pursuit. Like many farms in the valley, Eduardo's was a family enterprise. A generation back, his father, José, had bought five acres from Hiram Hadley for $500. That five acres eventually grew to five farms--one for each of José's children.

Jamie Stull, who returned home after more than four years in Burma and India, also took up his father's business--buying and developing land. During the depression Earl Stull, Sr. halfheartedly had paid $5 an acre to the El Paso Mortgage Company for 600 acres of mesa land at the eastern edge of town. Unlike Pat Garrett, he liked goats and thought about turning the mesa into a goat ranch. Instead, he sold some of the land to a housing developer. Another chunk of the would-be goat ranch eventually became the site for the Mesilla Valley Mall.

When Orville Priestley moved to Las Cruces in 1947 to become the publisher of the *Las Cruces Sun-News,* he found only two houses for sale and none to rent. Wartime shortages had made housing so scarce that some families resorted to camping along the riverbank. However, developers like Jamie Stull soon helped relieve the shortage. By the early 1950s he had a dozen builders working full time just to keep up with the demand.

Everyone, it seemed, also needed a new car. A month after

***Plaster curlicues** and wooden vigas (previous pages) stand above modern metal awnings as architectural reminders of the old downtown. The awnings shade customers visiting the farmers market on a bright Saturday morning.*

An aerial view *(above) of Las Cruces shows the location of the many landmarks before urban renewal in the 1960s. Looking north toward the Doña Ana Mountains, Loretto Academy is visible low and to the right of the center. The large white building, left of center, is the county courthouse. Just above and to the right of the courthouse is the Amador Hotel, with St. Genevieve's Church visible directly above the hotel on the east side of Main Street.*

the war ended, Rio Grande Motors announced it had reserved a percentage of its new cars for returning veterans, but would consider sales to others if ''the rate of (the soldiers') discharge is too slow.'' Some customers were so eager for a new car that they offered to pay the sticker price plus $1,000 or $2,000 in cash.

Las Cruces turned a hundred years old in 1949 and the city was ready to celebrate. An enthusiastic Centennial Committee sold stock in the event and with part of the $150,000 investment, hired a Hollywood troupe to design the sets and costumes. The celebration lasted a week and included a grandiose pageant called ''La Gran Fiesta'' staged at the college football stadium. However, the committee nearly lost its investment when two hours before showtime, a windstorm roared across the field, knocking down sets and sending the organizers into a frenzy. In true community spirit, however, the whole town pitched in to rebuild the set. And the show went on--all 17 episodes! The pageant had more than 1,000 participants, including 35 horsemen in Episode 10 alone. The Chicken Coop Dancers performed, bands played, and 29 young women competed for pageant queen.

In 1949, talk of Ovida ''Cricket'' Coogler replaced war stories at every coffee shop and cantina. Not since the Fountain murder had the valley been party to such a mystery. On Easter Sunday the body of the 18-year-old Coogler was found in a makeshift grave south of Las

Doña Ana County Sheriff *Miguel Apodaca (center) and deputies Santos Ramírez (left) and John Ault (right) smashed slot machines and other confiscated gambling paraphernalia in 1941. The resulting scrap metal was donated to the federal government for the war effort, and the $95 in nickels, dimes, and quarters that flowed from the demolished machines bought new sirens and fingerprinting equipment for local law enforcement agencies.*

Cruces. The young waitress had been missing 17 days. Two days after her body was found, Sheriff "Happy" Apodaca arrested Wesley Byrd, a black army veteran who had been seen at the DeLuxe Cafe where Coogler worked. He also arrested Jerry Nuzum, a former New Mexico A&M football star who had been with Coogler earlier on the evening she disappeared. However, Byrd was never charged with the crime and a judge dismissed the case against Nuzum without it going to a jury.

Oddly, Cricket Coogler's death was the catalyst that eventually exposed widespread gambling and corruption in New Mexico. Illegal gambling, using mostly slot machines, flourished openly in the state in the 1940s. Public officials from the local level on up were said to be receiving payoffs from gamblers in exchange for protection. However, Sheriff Apodaca, the only official tried for permitting gambling, was not convicted. Outraged over Apodaca's handling of the Coogler case, 300 students, faculty and townspeople petitioned for a grand jury investigation. (Among other things, Apodaca tortured Byrd, for which the sheriff and two deputies spent 10 months in a federal prison.)

When the grand jury realized that the corruption surrounding the Coogler case also extended to gambling, it launched a campaign against illegal gambling. Grand jury raiding parties hit casinos, clubs, lodges and veterans' halls confiscating a mountain of gambling equipment which they ceremoniously burned in front of the courthouse. As a result of their crusade, 52 people were indicted for gambling and liquor violations.

Although Coogler's death remains a mystery, old-timers speculate that she was involved with prominent politicians and that her death was accidental. The crime, they say, was in the cover up.

When Las Cruces emerged from its post-war catch-up period, it had become a full-fledged city with a new economic mainstay--defense technology. During the war, White Sands Proving Ground, as it was then called, remained remote and secretive, precisely the reasons the government selected the site in the first place.

New Mexico had been a favorite testing ground for rockets since Robert H. Goddard came to Roswell in 1930. Back in Massachusetts his rocket testing had impressed neither his neighbors nor the state fire marshall. Through Charles Lindbergh's help, Goddard received an $18,000 annual grant enabling him to continue his research in New Mexico. When they arrived in Roswell, Goddard and his

***Maj. Herbert L. Karsch,** proof officer, made a last minute inspection of the base of a V-2 rocket before it was fired from what was then the U.S. Army Ordnance Proving Ground at White Sands. In all, 67 V-2 rockets were assembled and tested at White Sands between 1946 and 1952. One series of tests called the "Blossom Project" carried out the first biological experiments in space.*

assistants quickly set up shop fashioning rockets from bicycle and automobile parts. Then from a lonely spot on the Mescalero ranch north of town, they launched the rockets from 60-foot towers into New Mexico's wide open spaces. Although the U.S. military during World War II saw little use for rockets, the Germans used Goddard's ideas and turned them into real weapons. In one six-month period, the Germans produced some 3,000 V-2 rockets, which they used to terrorize London and Europe.

By the fall of 1944 the United States had decided the V-2 had merit and officials were sent looking for a site to develop and test the missiles. The perfect place, they found, was New Mexico's sparsely settled Tularosa Basin, which was roughly the size of Connecticut. Since the early 1940s the army had used part of the area as a bombing range, much to the consternation of the ranchers in the area. Eventually the government condemned nearly all the ranches in the basin for military use.

In a turnabout Goddard would have appreciated, 300 railroad cars of German V-2 components that had been captured in Europe arrived in New Mexico in August 1945. For 20 days, freight cars carrying rocket parts unloaded at Las Cruces. From there army vehicles and nearly every flatbed truck in Doña Ana County were used to transport the components to the east side of the Organ Mountains. The *Las Cruces Sun-News* assured worried residents there was "no fear from explosions of the big V-2's swarming into town on Santa Fe freight cars."

More valuable than the rockets were the 200 German and Austrian rocket scientists who also had been captured during the war. Security officials carefully screened the scientists and placed paper clips on the personnel file folders of the 100 who had been selected to come to the United States to work in the missile program. The "paperclip crew" was headed by the famous Wernher Von Braun. By 1947 American scientists replaced the Germans in the test program, and although a few returned home, the majority remained in this country to become American citizens. In the late 1950s, Von Braun was the director of the Army's Ballistic Missile Program.

SUNDAY NIGHT

Under a banana moon the sky is fading
I can hear from my back yard
traffic along Solano Avenue. A siren.
A sad, rich, howling freight train
from Mesilla Park. Children's squeals.
A motorcycle's escalating drone. Spurts
of life everywhere in town after a typical
placid Sunday afternoon. Beause tonight
the weekend's over, folks. Have your one last
burst before we fall back down
to work and order Monday morning.

JOSEPH SOMOZA

Despite assurances from the newspaper, however, the V-2 was not failsafe. On one test firing in 1947, the 46-foot missile took off as planned but headed south to El Paso instead of north into the missile range. In the confusion, the rocket was allowed to fly over El Paso and Juárez, where a fiesta was in progress, and landed on a barren hill in a cemetery. Enterprising Mexicans roped off the crater, charged admission and sold bits of the V-2 as souvenirs.

As the Cold War heated up in the early 1950s, the pace of defense research at White Sands accelerated. By then the city and the college had taken an active interest in the missile range. The range provided government and civilian jobs for veterans, students and women, as well as the sons and daughters of farmers.

When the Russians launched Sputnik in October 1957, the pace quickened again. The educational system was challenged to produce more trained scientists. With his finger on the national pulse, President Roger Corbett announced his "Big Plan" to improve the college (including its football team) and increase enrollment. His first priority was the push to change the college's name to New Mexico State University to reflect its broader educational scope. Since Corbett's announcement in 1957, the university has grown from 2,600 students to a 1992 enrollment of 15,345. That year NMSU ranked 64th in the nation in federal research grants to colleges and universities.

Scientists who came to work at the missile range brought their families and as often as not settled in Las Cruces, adding yet another layer to the city's social and economic foundation. In 1992, nearly 10,000 people worked at White Sands Missile Range, making it Doña Ana County's largest and most lucrative employer.

By 1960 everything from babies to business was "boom, boom, boom." In the ten years

***J.H. Paxton** (right) served as Las Cruces mayor from 1920-1922. He was elected from and by the city council, which also included E.T. Winters, Charles Hill, Juan Lucero, C.O. Bennett, and A.F. Barncastle. In 1991, Ruben Smith became the first full-time mayor elected at large. The city operates under a city council, city manager form of government.*

since 1950, the population of Las Cruces had grown from 12,000 to more than 29,000. Las Cruces had been so busy expanding, however, that it had neglected its downtown, where familiar landmarks had been left to crumble. But business and civic leaders had no thoughts of abandoning the downtown. Instead, they decided to reshape it.

Frank Papen, had come to Las Cruces in 1940 to sell insurance. Before long the firm of Papen and Weisenhorn Insurance was the largest in the state. It numbered among its customers the Diocese of El Paso, which under the leadership of Bishop Sidney Metzger also included Las Cruces. In 1952 Papen joined the First National Bank's board of directors. Eventually, Papen came to control both the board and the bank.

By 1959 the 47-year-old-bank had outgrown its building on Main Street and Papen began looking for a new location. Bishop Metzger offered him the St. Genevieve's property for $126,000. The bishop considered St. Genevieve's obsolete, and intended to rebuild the church on Loretto Academy property. But public outcry against the sale of the old church quickly had Papen rethinking the deal. He cut the bank's losses and backed down. For a time the church had been reprieved.

The bank then turned its attention to the old Loretto Academy located at the south end of Main St. The academy, which had been abandoned by the Franciscan fathers, suffered further indignity when a truck failed to negotiate a turn and crashed into its walls. Eventually the Cruces Investment Company, of which Papen was a founder, bought the entire Loretto Academy property, including the historic Armijo House. The academy was demolished and Main

St. was realigned. The new two-story bank opened for business on the old Loretto site in 1962. Three years later Loretto Mall, the state's first enclosed, air-conditioned shopping center was built on the property. Later, Papen would add a 10-story modernistic bank tower, which to this day remains the tallest building in Las Cruces.

In a pattern that would be repeated nationwide, creation of the new mall caused an almost immediate decline in the down-town area. When urban renewal came along, the city's civic and business leaders had high hopes for rejuvenating downtown. Using millions of dollars in urban renewal funds they planned to reshape the downtown area into a modern, efficient city center. The massive project involved moving or refurbishing more than 160 businesses. Structures not directly related to business activities were demolished, including a whole neighborhood of adobe homes, and finally, St. Genevieve's. Main St. was turned into a pedestrian mall, complete with winding yellow brick path and angular metal awnings. What had been St. Genevieve's shaded courtyard spent time as a parking lot until Western Bank finally built on the site.

Caught up in good intentions and federal money, Las Cruces, along with the diocese, had succeeded in destroying the architectural heart of its city. The Hispanic community especially mourned the loss of its church, while others realized only too late their own attachment to the historic landmark. Mesilla, which had spent the last century noisily tending to its own business, chose not to participate in urban renewal. With the wisdom of hindsight plus strict zoning laws, Mesilla today looks like a spruced up version of its historic self.

During the late-1960s the nation was mired in an unpopular war, Tom Wolfe had chronicled the drug scene in The Electric Kool-Aid Acid Test, and the land-grant rebel Reies Tijerina was being tried on assault charges in a courthouse in Las Cruces. A year earlier Tijerina, along with 350 members of the group Alianza, had occupied a National Park campground near Santa Fe demanding restitution of Spanish

The Armijo House *was the first of its kind in Las Cruces with electrical wiring and a two-story addition constructed with three-foot thick walls. Nestor Armijo purchased the original large, four-room adobe house from Maricita Daily in 1877. The building later became the home of Josephine Gallagher, one of Nestor Armijo's granddaughters.*

community land grants. Now, he and five of his followers were on trial before Judge Howard C. Bratton for assaulting two U.S. Forest Rangers during the takeover. After the guilty verdict, Tijerina admitted to staging the takeover to draw public attention to their cause and bring matters to court.

However, the turmoil that engulfed the nation and parts of northern New Mexico barely grazed Las Cruces. As a whole, the town preferred to watch these debates from the sidelines. But when controversy did flare up, it did as it had everywhere--on campus.

"We hope by injecting a measure of controversy (and reality) into campus life," wrote the editors of the underground newspaper, "to make (NMSU) a somewhat more interesting university." After reporting on the increase of mini-skirts on campus (by a factor of five -- "Magnificent!"), further issues of the *Conscience* announced the scheduled appearance of Tijerina (who failed to show) and plans to form a chapter of Students for a Democratic Society. The paper ran photographs of a protest march from campus to the local draft board.

The administration was decidedly nervous and set up a long-range camera surveillance of those frequenting "The Hut," an off-campus coffee house. The president ordered the university police to confiscate copies of the paper. Its editors were fired from their campus jobs, and the earnest but irreverent paper finally was shut down. "We did not want the 60s campus of Berkeley on the New Mexico State campus," one administrator said. "We made sure it didn't happen."

Then in February 1973 frustration over rigid housing policies suddenly erupted into a student riot. At a time when other campuses were allowing students more freedom, NMSU still enforced a sign-in, sign-out policy for female students and an 11:00 p.m. curfew. When the Board of Regents abruptly canceled a trial "Intervisitation"

Green chiles, *purple earrings, custom cabinets, and crocheted caps -- plus more than 100 other homemade, homegrown specialties are for sale at the Las Cruces Farmers and Crafts Market on the Downtown Mall. Since its beginnings in 1971, the market has become a popular shopping tradition Wednesday and Saturday mornings.*

program, which allowed male and female students to visit in their rooms during set hours, the students gathered in protest at a women's dormitory. At first, student leaders were able to calm and disburse the agitated crowd. But the students gathered again outside, this time pelting campus police with rocks and bottles and smashing a police car window. About 75 police reinforcements arrived, fired tear gas into the mob, and arrested two students. The students persisted the next night with more rock throwing, and built a barricade of logs and broken concrete across Locust Street. State and local police, 180 strong, arrived in buses, and cleared the protesters out with tear gas. By Friday night a combination of the tear gas, snowy weather and behind-the-scenes discussions finally extinguished the demonstrations. Intervisitation was quietly reinstated in 1979.

While the 1970s was an impatient time for the city's young people, for Carmen Freudenthal it would be the culmination of 32 years of persistence. In 1940 when she became president of the Women's Improvement Association, an organization founded in 1894, she launched a drive to revise the state's community property laws. The proposed revision would allow married women the right to leave their estate to anyone they designated. At the time, only husbands had that right. For more than three decades, she and other women struggled to get the legislation passed. New Mexico's community property law finally was revised with the passage of the Equal Rights Amendment in 1972.

Carmen Sylva Henriette Kahn was born in Sedalia, Missouri, in 1898, to a Jewish family of comfortable means. After graduation from Smith College and stints working at a settlement house in Chicago and sales in St. Louis, she moved to New York City. There during the depths of the Depression, the persuasive young woman sold so many sets of encyclopedias that before long she was living on Park Avenue. On New Year's Day in 1930 she met a young man from a pioneer Las Cruces family and by March she and Louis Freudenthal were married and heading for New Mexico.

Here she quickly put her talents to work in a variety of community activities. She also made the local paper for wearing white satin pajamas at a party! In addition to her work on behalf of community property rights for women, she also established a prenatal and well-baby clinic, organized the Community Action Agency, formed a hospital auxiliary, helped open the first Planned Parenthood Clinic in southern New Mexico and helped

Thoroughly modern Carmen *Freudenthal was visiting San Francisco in 1932 when Dorothea Lang took this photograph. By that time the former Carmen Kahn had married Louis Freudenthal and moved to New Mexico. He was president of the New Mexico Farm Bureau; she was a child labor law activist. By the mid-1930s Lang also was in New Mexico with the Farm Security Administration photographing the plight of local farm families and drought refugees passing through on their way to California.*

organize the Community Concert Association.

Carmen Freudenthal, who came of age just as women received the right to vote, helped give voice to the needs of women and children in New Mexico. That she also used her talents to benefit Las Cruces is a tribute to both the woman and the community she loved.

In 1980 an old feud between neighbors was ignited when El Paso sued New Mexico for access to ground water inside the New Mexico state line. The $17 million contest would last more than a decade. At stake was New Mexico's authority to control its water resources. El Paso, in its search for more water to supply a population that would reach 504,000 by 1990, found a cheap and abundant source just across the state line in New Mexico. The city planned to drill wells in two New Mexico locations and pipe the water into El Paso. The only obstacle was a New Mexico law prohibiting export of ground

Hot air balloons *of peculiar design added a whimsical note to the Las Cruces skyline during the 1993 Mesilla Valley Balloon Rally. The rally attracted some 60 balloons to the January event.*

The tuba section *(left) of the Oñate High School marching band step in time during practice for a 1992 band competition in Dallas. The newest of the city's three high schools, Oñate moved from its temporary location at a junior high school to its newly completed $22 million facility in September 1993.*

These medieval youngsters *had their faces painted at one of the 150 arts and crafts booths at the Renaissance Craftfaire. More than 50,000 people attended the 1992 fair, which featured food booths, strolling musicians, and a huge dragon floating in a lagoon.*

Hiram Hadley, *the founder and first president of what is now New Mexico State University, was photographed in the early 1900s while watering his trees in front of his "Home Place." Hadley built his house in 1907 near the college, on what is now the corner of El Paseo and University Avenue. He grew pears, apples, and grapes on his four-acre property.*

Texan Jim Hightower (center) rallied a partisan crowd awaiting the arrival of vice presidential candidate Albert Gore less than a week before the 1992 election. Because New Mexico was a swing state, representatives of both parties gave Las Cruces unaccustomed attention during the campaign.

water outside the state. On Sept. 5, El Paso sued to overturn New Mexico's water export ban as unconstitutional. El Paso reasoned, and the courts later agreed, that water should be treated as any other commodity and as such should be freely transported across state lines.

People in the Mesilla Valley were both shocked and outraged by El Paso's surprise move. The state of New Mexico, Las Cruces, Doña Ana County, the irrigation district and the university, in addition to other communities and groups affected by such a water transfer quickly joined forces against El Paso.

By the time it was over, New Mexico's export ban had been overturned, new water laws had been written, and El Paso still was denied the water. Exhausted by court battles and tired of animosity, both sides finally agreed to a settlement in May 1991. The agreement called for both sides to drop their lawsuits and for the formation of a joint commission where they would work out their water problems.

Wars and water battles aside, the people of this valley have

Quinceañera Lené Saucedo *(above right) and her escort Robert Romero were presented at her Quinceañera dance, one of the events celebrating her fifteenth birthday in 1992. The coming-of-age tradition featured 15 attendants and their escorts as well as various religious and social events.*

held to a common tradition--they love to entertain themselves. In Tortugas, dancers still perform their solemn cadence wearing the high crowned headdresses of their Aztec ancestors. On the plaza in Mesilla fiestas still begin with the brassy fanfare of a mariachi band. And in an old section of Las Cruces, a men's choir in western shirts and red string ties, returns each Christmas to fill St. Paul's Methodist Church with their rich voices.

Add to these, the lyric opera, the symphony, the ballet, the community chorus, and bands, bands, bands of every size and sound. In fine tradition, the Fountain Theater shows classic, foreign and art films sponsored by the Mesilla Valley Film Society, while both the community and the university theaters produce full playbills each season. NMSU resident playwright Mark Medoff premiered his Tony Award winning *Children of a Lesser God* in Las Cruces in 1979.

Artists, writers, poets and potters occupy a less noisy place in the cultural life of Las Cruces. Art galleries thrive near the plaza in Mesilla. In downtown Las Cruces the city's gracious old adobe library has been converted into the Branigan Cultural Center where paintings and photographs share space with quilt exhibits and art classes. Expansion plans will include more space for historical exhibits. The university boasts an art gallery and a museum, both offering traveling exhibits as well as local collections. With the help of the state legislature, a long-dreamed of Farm and Ranch Heritage Museum appears close to realization.

The Mesilla Valley has long provided a creative landscape for writers like Denise Cháves, author of *Last of the Menu Girls,* and poets like Keith Wilson, who wrote *Lion's Gate.*

Las Cruces thrives in this varied cultural climate thanks in part to its aggressive arts council, which is the largest in the state. The Doña Ana Arts Council and its regiment of volunteers each year put on the Renaissance Craftfaire and the Arte Picante arts and crafts show. In addition to a dizzying variety of sponsored activities, the council also supports the Hispanic Arts Council and the Exceptional Artists Cooperative.

Efforts at historical preservation, however, are not as well organized. The city made a good start in 1982 when it co-sponsored the Las Cruces Historic Buildings Survey. As a result, both the Alameda Depot District and the Mesquite Original Townsite District have since been included on the National Register of Historic Places. At the time the city also considered creating an Historical Preservation Board. But the board was never formed and the city's activities since then have been limited to issuing historic building plaques.

Historical preservation at the grassroots level is divided among a loose network of associations, societies and neighborhood groups. The lesson of St. Genevieve's has not been lost on them, as they strive for more recognition and clout.

The commercial sector has had a major role in historic preservation. In 1982, Pioneer Savings and Trust, with help from grant-in-aid funds from the New Mexico Historical Preservation Bureau, restored the Armijo House for its branch office. (It has since been converted to law offices.) Nestor Armijo was a prosperous businessman and rancher during the heyday of the Santa Fe Trail. In 1877 Armijo bought the adobe house, which he enlarged and furnished in elaborate Victorian style. Over the next 100 years, six generations of the Armijo family lived in the house.

Citizens Bank likewise restored the old Amador Hotel to its former showplace status. Since then, however, the bank has outgrown the location and the county uses the former hotel for its office annex. Jeweler Glenn Cutter recently bought Hiram Hadley's home, which until lately served as a fraternity house.

Cutter has remodeled the two-story home for use as a jewelry store.

Cooperation with the state has led to the designation of Fort Selden as a state park. Nearly every weekend, the old fort comes alive with activities from military reenactments to adobe construction demonstrations. A more complicated transaction in 1988 led to the preservation of both Van Patten's old Dripping Springs health resort and the environmental protection of the Organ Mountains. A.B. Cox, one of W.W. Cox's rancher sons, bought the property in 1957. After A.B. died in 1975 the family began discussions with the U.S. Bureau of Land Management on how to protect the mountain range from development. Finally, through a series of land exchanges and purchases, the Cox Ranch has become part of the 30,000-acre Organ Mountain Recreation Area. The recreation area is jointly managed by the BLM and The Nature Conservancy, a non-profit group dedicated to preserving unique wild lands.

Those who live here are rightly concerned with the effects of growth on the valley and its mountains. Las Cruces, the second largest city in New Mexico, is projected to continue its 2.2 percent growth rate to the year 2000 when the population is expected to reach 80,000. The defense industry will continue its important role in employment and

A mural *on a retaining wall near Young Park was painted by students from the Native American Preparatory School. The mural tradition is well-represented in Las Cruces where murals decorate high schools, water tanks, walls and amphitheaters.*

income into the next century, as will agriculture and education. The lack of broad-based employment, however, probably will continue to hold the city's per capita income near the state average of $11,246, according to the 1990 census. The completion of a border crossing in southern Doña Ana County, along with the implementation of a free trade zone with Mexico, is expected to create much needed jobs in that area in the future.

Hispanics made up 47 percent of the city's population in 1990, a figure that may decline as more Anglos choose Las Cruces for their retirement homes. Blacks made up 2 percent of the Las Cruces population, twice that of the Native American population, a trend that also can be expected to continue. However, it is hazardous to predict such trends considering the city's proximity to Mexico and its Hispanic heritage.

The lure of land and water that brought the first colonists to this valley is as strong today as it was 150 years ago. It is the landscape that holds people here, that gives them a sense of place.

It is a place where a country road travels for miles alongside shaded rows of pecan trees, where the croplands of the legendary Doña Ana now produce more cotton, more vegetables, and more farm income than any county in the state. Here the ancient Rio Grande once wild and loopy now conforms to the slight curves of a manmade channel. And not far away on the back streets of Mesilla, adobe homes crowd behind the plaza. Less than 2,000 people live there now.

It is a place where a city of 62,000 still feels like a hometown. Where an irrigation ditch cuts down the center of Main Street, and cotton blooms in a field across from Las Cruces High School. Where early morning commuters face the sunrise on their way to White Sands Missile Range, and Saturday night fans fill the freeway headed to a university concert.

It is a place where history is measured by the generation. Here, a great-great-great grandson of Simon Enriquez prospers growing chile on the family farm, while Fountain grandchildren run businesses in Mesilla and a Freudenthal granddaughter crusades to save the railroad depot.

And it's a place where its people are inseparable from their landscape. Where the highway stretches to the western horizon, where city lights fill the valley, and orchards follow the river. And where climbers dare challenge the granite spires of the Organ Mountains.

CREDITS

ART/ILLUSTRATIONS

Fred Chilton: Dust Jacket Cover

Samuel W. Cozzens, from *The Marvelous Country,* 1873: 12-13

Bob Diven, courtesy First National Bank of Doña Ana County: 28-29, 46, 53

John Hughes, from *Doniphan's Expedition,* 1848: 34

Joseph Ireland: Endsheets, 14 (from a photograph by the Doña Ana County Archaeological Society)

Las Casas, from *History of America*, 1884: 22

Rio Grande Historical Collections, New Mexico State University Library: 24, 36-37, 78

Rio Grande Historical Collections, New Mexico State University Library, from *Andrew Belcher Gray Report:* 31, 45, 50

Rogers, from *Harper's Magazine,* 1880: 17

PHOTOGRAPHS

Ilsa Altshool: 92, 102, 118 (Dorothea Lang photograph)

Russell Bamert: Color Transparencies for Dust Jacket Cover and Endsheets

City of Las Cruces: 114

Victor Espinoza: Dust Jacket Portrait, 122
Hobson-Huntsinger University Archives, New Mexico State University Library: 76, 77, 87 (top), 120 (bottom)

Las Cruces Public Schools: 97 (top)

National Archives: 42 (top)

Pamela Porter: 10-11, 26-27, 38-39, 60-61, 82-83, 106-107

Permanent Collection of New Mexico State University Museum: 30

Rio Grande Historical Collections, New Mexico State University Library: 19, 23, 32, 33, 40-41, 42 (bottom), 43, 44, 48, 52, 54, 55, 56, 58-59, 62-63, 63, 64, 67, 68, 69, 70, 71, 72, 73, 74, 75, 79, 80, 81, 84-85, 86, 87 (bottom), 88, 89, 90, 91, 93, 94, 97 (bottom), 98, 100, 103, 104, 105, 108-109, 110, 115

Cheryl Thornburg of the *Las Cruces Bulletin:* 116, 119, 120 (top), 121, 124

U.S. Bureau of Land Management property in the Permanent Collection of the New Mexico State University Museum: 16

White Sands Missile Range: 112

POEMS

Alice W. Gruver: 35

Nancy Peters Hastings, from *Orphic Lute,* 1992: 65

Margaret Page Hood, from *History of Mesilla Valley:* 51

Joseph Somoza, from *Backyard Poems,* Cinco Puntos Press: 113

Gaspar Pérez de Villagrá, from *Historia de la Nueva México, 1610,* University of New Mexico Press: 20

Keith Wilson, from *Lion's Gate,* Cinco Puntos Press: 96

BIBLIOGRAPHY

BOOKS

Ayer, Edward E. Mrs., trans. *The Memorial of Fray Alonso de Benavides.* Albuquerque: Horn and Wallace, 1965.

Barrick, Nona, and Mary Taylor. *The Mesilla Guard: 1851-61.* Monograph No. 51. El Paso: Texas Western Press, 1976.

Beck, Warren A. *New Mexico: A History of Four Centuries.* Norman: University of Oklahoma Press, 1962.

Beckett, Patrick H., and Terry L. Corbett. "The Manso Indians." Monograph No. 9. Las Cruces: Coas Publishing, 1992.

_____________. "Tortugas." Monograph No. 8. Las Cruces: Coas Publishing, 1990.

Blawis, Patricia Bell. *Tijerina and the Land Grants: Mexican American Struggle for Their Heritage.* New York: International Publishers, 1971.

Blum, John M., Edmund S. Morgan, Willie Lee Rose, Arthur M. Schlesinger, Jr., Kenneth M. Stampp, and C. Vann Woodward. *The National Experience: Part One A History of the United States to 1877.* New York: Harcourt Brace Jovanovich, Inc., 1981.

_____________. *The National Experience: Part Two A History of the United States Since 1865.* New York: Harcourt Brace Jovanovich, Inc., 1981.

Bolton, Herbert Eugene. *Coronado, Knight of Pueblos and Plains.* Albuquerque: University of New Mexico Press, 1949.

Bruun, Geoffrey. *Survey of European Civilization, Part II.* 4th ed. Boston: Houghton Mifflin Co., 1964.

Buchanan, Rosemary. *The First Hundred Years.* Las Cruces: Bronson Printing Co., Inc., 1961.

Chegin, Rita Kasch. *Survivors: Women of the Southwest.* Las Cruces: Yucca Tree Press, 1991.

Chronic, Halka. *Roadside Geology of New Mexico.* Missoula: Mountain Press Publishing Co., 1987.

Clark, Ira G. *Water in New Mexico: A History of Its Management and Use*. Albuquerque: University of New Mexico Press, 1987.

Cohrs, Timothy. *Fort Selden, New Mexico.* Santa Fe: State Monuments Division Museum of New Mexico, 1974.

Conkling, Roscoe P., and Margaret B. Conkling. *The Butterfield Overland Mail 1857-1869. Vol. 1, 1.* Glendale: Arthur H. Clark Co., 1947.

Davis, W.W.H. *El Gringo: New Mexico and Her People.* New York: Harper and Bros. Reprint Bison Books, 1982.

Donaldson, Edith. *History of Public Education within the Gadsden I.S. District.* National Education Association. 1957.

Ellis, Richard N. *New Mexico Historic Documents.* Albuquerque: University of New Mexico Press, 1975.

_____________. ed. *New Mexico Past and Present: A Historic Reader.* Albuquerque: University of New Mexico Press, 1971.

Fierman, Floyd S. *Some Early Jewish Settlers on the Southwestern Frontier.* El Paso: Texas Western Press, 1960.

Frost, H. Gordon. *The Gentlemen's Club: The Story of Prostitution in El Paso.* El Paso: Mangan Books, 1983.

Granjon, Henry. *Along the Rio Grande.* Michael Romero Taylor, ed. Albuquerque: University of New Mexico Press, 1986.

Great Events of the 20th Century: How They Changed Our Lives. Pleasantville: The Reader's Digest Assn., Inc., 1977.

Griggs, George. *A History of the Mesilla Valley; or The Gadsden Purchase.* N.p., 1930.

Grun, Bernard. *The Timetables of History.* New York: Simon and Schuster, 1979.

Hadley, Anna R., Carlone H. Allen, and C. Frank Allen. *Hiram Hadley.* Privately printed. 1924.

Hall, Linda B. and Don M. Coerver. *Revolution on the Border: The United States and Mexico 1910 - 1920.* Albuquerque: University of New Mexico Press, 1988.

Hammond, George P., ed. *Revolt of the Pueblo Indians of New Mexico and Otermín's attempted Reconquest 1680-1682. Vol. 8 (1).* Albuquerque: University of New Mexico Press, 1942.

Horgan, Paul. *Lamy of Santa Fe.* New York: Farrar, Strauss and Girous, 1975.

Hsi, David, and Janda Panitz, eds. *From Sundaggers to Space Exploration--Significant Scientific Contributions to Science and Technology in New Mexico.* Special Issue of the New Mexico Journal of Science. Vol. 26, No. 1, February 1986.

Jarratt, B. Franklin. *Seen Through the Eyes of a Button*. El Paso: Guynes Printing Co., 1977.

Jensen, Joan M., and Darlis A. Miller, eds. *New Mexico Women: Intercultural Perspectives.* Albuquerque: University of New Mexico Press. 1986.

Kapp, Anne E., and Guylyn Nusom, eds. *The Las Cruces Historic Buildings Survey.* Las Cruces: City of Las Cruces, n.d.

Koury, Phil A. *Treasure of Victoria Peak.* Pennsylvania: Schiffer Publishing Ltd., 1986.

Kropp, Simon F. *That All May Learn.* Las Cruces: New Mexico State University, 1972.

Lane, Lydia Spencer. *I Married a Soldier.* Albuquerque: University of New Mexico Press, 1987.

Larson, Robert W. *New Mexico's Quest for Statehood 1846 - 1912.* Albuquerque: University of New Mexico Press, 1968.

Lisle, Ruth J. *Chickens Don't Turn to Dust.* Philadelphia: Dorrance & Company, 1968.

Lydick, Jess, with Paula Ruth Moore. *One Man's Word: A Seven Decade Personal American History.* Las Cruces: Nightjar Press, 1990.

Magoffin, Susan Shelby. *Down the Santa Fe Trail and into Mexico.* Lincoln: University of Nebraska Press, 1982.

Mangan, Frank. *El Paso in Pictures.* El Paso: The Press, 1971.

Marshall, Michael P. "Background Information on the Jornada Culture Area." In *Survey of the Tularosa Basin.* Las Cruces: Human Systems Research, Inc., 1973.

Matson, Eva Jane, compiled 2nd ed. *Heroes of Bataan Coregidor and Northern Luzon.* Las Cruces: Yucca Tree Press, 1989.

McKee, James Cooper. *Narrative of the Surrender of a Command of U.S. Forces at Fort Fillmore, New Mexico in July A.D. 1861.* Houston: Stagecoach Press, 1960.

McMahon, Iona Ellis, and Eva Jane Matson. "A History of the Methodist Church in Las Cruces, New Mexico." N.p., n.d.

Metz, Leon P. *Southern New Mexico Empire: The First National Bank of Doña Ana County.* El Paso: Mangan Books, 1991.

________________. *Desert Army: Fort Bliss on the Texas Border.* El Paso: Mangan Books, 1988.

________________. *Pat Garrett: The Story of a Western Lawman.* Norman: University of Oklahoma Press, 1974.

Meyer, Michael C. and William L. Sherman. *The Course of Mexican History* (4th Ed.). New York: Oxford University Press, 1991.

Miller, Darlis A. *Soldiers and Settlers: Military Supply in the Southwest.* Albuquerque: University of New Mexico Press, 1989.

________________. *The California Column in New Mexico.* Albuquerque: University of New Mexico Press, 1982.

Myrick, David F. *New Mexico Railroads: A Historical Survey.* Albuquerque: University of New Mexico Press, 1970.

Opler, Morris E. "Mescalero Apache." In *Handbook of North American Indians.* Vol. 10. Alfonso Ortiz, vol. ed. Washington, D.C.: Smithsonian Institution, 1983.

Parkes, Henry Bamford. *A History of Mexico.* Boston: Houghton Mifflin Co., 1969.

Priestley, Lee. *Shalam: Utopia on the Rio Grande 1881-1907.* El Paso: Texas Western Press, 1988.

Rickards, Colin. *Sheriff Pat Garrett's Last Days.* Santa Fe: Sunstone Press, 1986.

Sale, Patrick. *The Conquest of Paradise: Christopher Columbus and the Columbian Legacy.* New York: Alfred A. Knopf, 1990.

Simmons, Marc. *The Las Conquistador.* Norman: University of Oklahoma Press, 1991.

________________. *Albuquerque.* Albuquerque: University of New Mexico Press, 1982.

________________. *New Mexico: An Interpretive History.* Albuquerque: University of New Mexico Press, 1977.

Sonnichsen, C.L. *Pass of the North: Four Centuries on the Rio Grande, Vol II.* El Paso: Texas Western Press, 1980.

________________. *The Mescalero Apaches.* Norman: University of Oklahoma Press, 1973.

________________. *Pass of the North: Four Centuries on the Rio Grande, Vol I.* El Paso: Texas Western Press, 1968.

________________. *Tularosa: Last of the Frontier West.* Albuquerque: University of New Mexico Press, 1960.

Spidle, Jake W., Jr. *Doctors of Medicine in New Mexico: A History of Health and Medical Practice 1886-1986.* Albuquerque: University of New Mexico Press, 1986.

Stuart, David E. *Glimpses of the Ancient Southwest.* Santa Fe: Ancient City Press, 1985.

Szasz, Ferenc Morton. *The Day the Sun Rose Twice.* Albuquerque: University of New Mexico Press, 1984.

Timmons, W.H. *El Paso: A Borderlands History.* El Paso: Texas Western Press, 1990.

Villagrá, Gaspar Pérez de. *Historia de las Nueva México, 1610.* Translated and edited by Miguel Encinas, Alfred Rodríguez, and Joseph P. Sánchez. Albuquerque: University of New Mexico Press, 1992.

Wiley, Tom. *Public School Education in New Mexico.* Albuquerque: Division of Government Research, University of New Mexico, 1965.

Williams, Jerry L., ed. *New Mexico in Maps.* Albuquerque: University of New Mexico Press, 1986.

Wilson, John P. *Merchants, Guns and Money: The Story of Lincoln County and Its Wars.* Santa Fe: Museum of New Mexico Press, 1987.

ARTICLES AND THESES

Basehart, Harry W. "Mescalero Apache Subsistence Patterns" In Survey of the Tularosa Basin. Las Cruces: Human Systems Research, Inc., 1973.

Bloom, Maude Elizabeth McFie. "A History of the Mesilla Valley." Master's thesis, New Mexico College of Agriculture and Mechanic Arts, June 1903.

Bowden, J. J. "Spanish and Mexican Land Grants in the Chihuahuan Acquisitions." El Paso: Texas Western Press, 1971.

Boyd, Douglas K., and Meeks Etchieson. "Historic Resources Related to Construction Activities at Elephant Butte Reservoir." Amarillo: U.S. Department of the Interior, Bureau of Reclamation, Southwest Region, August 1986.

Brown, Jeffrey P. "Temple Beth El of Las Cruces, New Mexico: The Early Years." Unpublished manuscript property of Jeffrey P. Brown, n.d.

Carpenter, James. "Las Cruces Public Schools Building History." Unpublished manuscript, Las Cruces Public School District. 1970.

"Centennial Celebration 1849-1949." Las Cruces: Centennial Corporation, 1949.

"Chronicle of Higher Education." 10 April 1991.

Clark, Ira G."The Elephant Butte Controversy: A Chapter in the Emergence of Federal Water Law." Journal of American History. Vol LXI, No. 4. March 1975.

Conlee, C.S. "Las Cruces Municipal Schools Handbook." N.p., n.d.

Creel, Bobby J., Linda G. Harris, Gary L. Bruner, Charles T. DuMars, John W. Hernandez, and Robert R. Lansford. "Water: Lifeblood of New Mexico." Las Cruces: New Mexico State University, 1988.

Doña Ana County School District No. 2 Board Minutes. 9 July 1904 to 1 July 1913.

Duran, Meliha S. "Patterns of Prehistoric Land Use in Doña Ana County, New Mexico." Report No. 471. Las Cruces: Cultural Resources Management Division, New Mexico State University, 1982.

______________. "Doña Ana County Archeology." Unpublished manuscript, property of Meliha S. Duran, n.d.

Hanley, Theresa M. "Stahmann Farms Migrant Community." Master's thesis work in progress, New Mexico State University.

Harris, Linda G., Robert C. Czerniak, Richard A. Earl, and William J. Gribb. "Whose Water Is It, Anyway?" Las Cruces: Arroyo Press, 1990.

"History of the Armijo House." Las Cruces: Pioneer Savings & Trust, n.d.

Kues, Barry S. and Jonathan F. Callendar. "Geologic History." In *New Mexico in Maps.* Albuquerque: University of New Mexico Press, 1986.

Kues, Barry S. "Mesozoic Paleontology." In *New Mexico in Maps.* Albuquerque: University of New Mexico Press, 1986.

"Land of Colorful Contrasts." Las Cruces: Las Cruces Convention and Visitors Bureau, n.d.

La Mar, Barbel Schoenfeld. "Water and Land in the Mesilla Valley, New Mexico: Reclamation and Its Effects on Property Ownership and Agricultural Land Use." Ph.D. dissertation., University of Oregon, 1984.

Larson, Robert W. "Struggle for Statehood." New Mexico Magazine. January 1987.

"Las Cruces Comprehensive Plan." Vol. 1, 2. Draft. Las Cruces: EDAW, Inc., 14 December 1983.

Lehmer, Donald J. "The Jornada Branch of the Mogollon." Social Science Bulletin No. 17. Vol. 14, No. 2. Tucson: University of Arizona, April 1948.

Lester, Paul A. "History of Elephant Butte Irrigation District." Master's thesis, New Mexico State University, July 1977.

"Living Authors of the Mesilla Valley." Las Cruces: Friends of Branigan Memorial Library, April 1991.

MacNeish, Richard S. "Defining the Archaic Chihuahua Tradition." Annual Report of the Andover Foundation for Archaeological Research. Andover: Andover Foundation for Archaeological Research, 1949.

Mickle, Robert. "Las Cruces in the 1940s: Impressions of a Few Residents." Unpublished manuscript, New Mexico State University Rio Grande Historical Collection. 16 April 1991.

Miller, Darlis A. "The Frontier Army in the Far West: 1860-1900." In The Forum Series. FA106. St. Louis: Forum Press, 1979.

Milton, Hugh M. "Land Grants of Doña Ana County, New Mexico." New Mexico State University Rio Grande Historical Collection. N.p., n.d.

Minter, Ilka Feather. "Philetus M. Thompson." Rio Grande History No. 14. New Mexico State University Rio Grande Historical Collection, 1983.

Neilson, John Craig. "Communidad: Community Life in a Southwestern Town, Las Cruces, New Mexico, 1880-1890." Master's thesis, New Mexico State University, 1988.

"New Mexico Agricultural Statistics 1989." Las Cruces: U.S. Department of Agriculture and New Mexico Department of Agriculture, 1989.

Pope, J. "Survey of the Mesilla Valley." Map. Washington, D.C.: U.S. Army Corps of Engineers, 1854.

"The Rise and Fall of a Conscience: Memories of Learning." New Mexico State University Television Production, 1988.

Sandoval, Raymond Edward. "Intrusion and Domination: A Study of the Relationship of Chicano Development to the Exercise and Distribution of Power in a Southwestern Community, 1870-1974." Ph.D. dissertation, University of Washington, 1980.

Singleton, Nena. "Jewel of the Organs: Historic Ranch Spared from City's Sprawl." New Mexico Magazine. February 1990.

Tod, Nancy. "Other Sides of Roy Nakayama: Origins, Creativity, and Committment." Unpublished manuscript. Presented to New Mexico Historical Society Conference April 20, 1991.

Thomas, Gerald W. "Memo to those interested in the recent student disturbances at New Mexico State University." 3 March 1973.

Trumbo, Theron M., ed. "The History of Las Cruces and the Mesilla Valley." Las Cruces: Historical Data Committee of the Centennial, 1949.

"White Sands Missile Range Fact Sheet, Statistics for Fiscal Year 1990." White Sands: White Sands Missile Range Public Information Office, 1990.

"White Sands Missile Range Fact Sheet, V-2 Story." White Sands: White Sands Missile Range Public Information Office, n.d.

Wilson, Clyde A., Robert R. White, Brennon R. Orr, and R. Gary Roybal. "Water Resources of the Rincon and Mesilla Valleys and Adjacent Areas, New Mexico." Technical Report 43. Santa Fe: U.S. Geological Survey and New Mexico State Engineer, 1981.

NEWSPAPERS

Conscience
El Paso Times
Las Cruces Bulletin
Las Cruces Citizen
Las Cruces Sun-News
Mesilla Miner
Mesilla Times
Rio Grande Farmer
Rio Grande Republican
Round Up
San Antonio Herald

INTERVIEWS

Altshool, Elsa. President, Doña Ana Historic Preservation Coalition. Telephone conversation with author, 4 June 1991.

Bean, Joyce. New Mexico State University graduate, 1919. Interview with author. Mesilla Park, New Mexico, 25 April 1991.

Clark, Ira G. Professor Emeritus, New Mexico State University. Interview with author. Mesilla Park, New Mexico, 23 April 1991.

Diven, William P. Former *El Paso Times* reporter. Telephone conversation with author, 4 June 1991.

Enriquez, Raymundo G. Retired farmer. Interview with author, Mesilla Park, New Mexico, 24 April 1991.

Fernandez, Eduardo. New Mexico State University graduate, 1940. Interview with author, South of Las Cruces, New Mexico, 22 April 1991.

Hawley, John W. Environmental geologist, New Mexico Bureau of Mines and Mineral Resources. Telephone conversation with author, 23 March 1990.

Kirkpatrick, David. Anthropologist, Human Systems Research, Inc. Interview with author. Mesilla, New Mexico, 13 February 1990.

Lydick, Jess. Retired businessman. Telephone conversation with author, 13 June 1991.

Pollard, Heather. Director, Doña Ana Arts Council. Interview with author. Las Cruces, New Mexico, 28 May 1991.

Priestley, Lee. Former publisher, *Las Cruces Sun-News.* Interview with author. Las Cruces, New Mexico, 28 May 1991.

Smiggen, Bob. Director, New Mexico State University Housing Office. Interview with author. Las Cruces, New Mexico, 5 June 1991.

Stull, Jamie. Real Estate developer and former member, Las Cruces City Council. Interview with author. Las Cruces, New Mexico, 22 April 1991.

Tomlin, Tommy. School teacher and former Las Cruces mayor. Interview with author. Las Cruces, New Mexico, 30 May 1991.

Traylor, Cal. Former president, Doña Ana County Historical Society. Telephone conversation with author, 21 June 1991.

White, Ken. Former Las Cruces city planner. Interview with author. Las Cruces, New Mexico, 29 May 1991.

Williams, James. Professor of Sociology and Anthropology, New Mexico State University. Telephone conversation with author, 1 May 1991.

Zaldo, Bruno. City Manager, Las Cruces. Telephone conversation with author, 5 June 1991.

CHRONOLOGY

900-1400 Inhabited by prehistoric Indians. Las Tules site inhabited.

1535 Nov. Alvar Nuñez Cabeza de Vaca, with a negro slave Estevan cross southern New Mexico, however his exact route is unknown.

1540-41 Francisco Vázquez de Coronado makes the first official Spanish expedition to the Southwest.

1581 Fray Augustin Rodriguez and Capt. Francisco Sánchez Chamuscado lead a small party of Spaniards up from Chihuahua.

1583 Jan. Antonio Espejo travels up the Rio Grande near Mesilla.

1598 Juan de Oñate passes through the Mesilla Valley on his way north to establish the first non-Indian settlement in the United States.

1605 Oñate mentions an Indian village, Trenequel de la Mesilla.

1610 Oñate's historian, Capt. Gaspar Pérez de Villagrá publishes *Historia de la Nueva México, 1610.*

1620 The first permanent colony in New England is established at Plymouth.

1624 Capt. John Smith publishes *General History of Virginia.*

1680 Aug. 10. The Pueblo Indians revolt, driving Gov. Antonio de Otermín to El Paso del Norte for refuge.

1692 Aug. 16. Don Diego de Vargas and his army depart El Paso to re-establish Spanish sovereignty in the North. The Camino Real resumes its importance as the main route from Chihuahua, Mexico to Santa Fe.

1790 Santa Teresa Spanish Land Grant is established in the lower Mesilla Valley near El Paso del Norte. Apache activity forces the closing of some of these ranches.

1798 Legend of Lost Padre Mine originates when a dying soldier tells Padre La Rue the location of gold in the Organ Mountains.

1805 Aug. 4. Brazito Spanish Land Grant is established. Also later closed due to Apache threat.

1810 Sept. 16. The "Grito de Dolores" launches the war for Mexican Independence.

1821 Aug. 27. Mexico gains independence from Spain and allows traders from the United States to trade with Mexican citizens.

1840 Aug. 5. Doña Ana Bend Colony Grant established with 35,399 acres. Colony formed Jan. 26, 1843.

1846 May 13. U.S. declares war with Mexico.

1846 Dec. 25. Battle of Brazito. Col. Alexander Doniphan and his troops defeat the Mexican Army in the only battle of the U.S.-Mexico War fought in New Mexico.

1848 Jan. 24. Gold is discovered in California.

1848 July 4. Treaty of Guadalupe-Hidalgo officially ends the Mexican-American War. Land east of the Rio Grande ceded to the U.S.; land west is disputed. Texans begin arriving in the Mesilla Valley to claim land.

1849 Las Cruces is founded. Lt. Delos Bennett Sackett of the Doña Ana garrison surveys the village and residents draw "suertes," or lots, to determine which property they would own. Population is 600.

1849 The Gold Rush attracts 80,000 "forty-niners" to California gold fields discovered in 1848.

1850 March 1. Rafael Ruelas and 60 Mexicans establish Mesilla on the Mexican west bank of the Rio Grande.

1850 Under the Compromise of 1850 California is admitted to the Union as a free state; New Mexico and Utah territories are created with no restriction on slavery; Texas boundary is fixed in its present form and the federal government pays the state $10,000 to withdraw land claims in New Mexico.

1850 Americans take the first census of Las Cruces (600 pop.) and Mesilla (3,000 pop.)

1851 Ft. Fillmore, south of present day Tortugas, is established to defend farmers and wagon trains against Apaches. The fort closes in 1862.

1851 The Stephenson mine is discovered by men searching for the Lost Padre Mine.

1852 Jan. 6. Doña Ana County is formed. Its boundaries stretch from Texas to California and include southern Arizona and New Mexico, some 300,000 sqare miles. Today it covers 3,840 square miles.

1852 Feb. 2, Refugio Colony Grant established. Aug. 3, Santo Tomas de Iturbide Grant is established. June 20, Mesilla Civil Colony Grant established.

1853 Signed Dec. 30 in Mexico City. The Gadsden Purchase establishes the present international boundary between Mexico and the United States. The U.S. pays Mexico $10 million for the 30,000 square-mile tract.

1858 Sept. 30. Butterfield Overland Mail reaches Mesilla, the largest town between San Antonio and California. The southern route of the Butterfield Stage is established with stations in Mesilla, Picacho, and Rough and Ready Hills.

1859 St. Genevieve's Catholic Church is built in Las Cruces.

1860 Oct. 18. *Mesilla Times,* first newspaper is published in the region. Publication ceases April 1862.

1860 Las Cruces population is 768, Mesilla, 2,420; El Paso, 428.

1861 July 25. Confederate Lt. Col. John R. Baylor invades, occupies Mesilla, which becomes the Confederate Capitol of Arizona. Union forces retreat, then surrender at San Augustín Pass on July 27.

1861 Nov. 4. First District Court session is held in Mesilla. First on the docket is the forclosure of the *Mesilla Times.*

1862 March 26. Union volunteers from Colorado defeat the Confederates in New Mexico and they retreat to Texas.

1862 Aug. 10. The California Column, Union volunteers, march from the west coast to Mesilla. The Confederates had already left and there is no fighting.

1862 Homestead Act allots 160 acres to settlers who live on the land for five years. In the arid West, two-thirds of the farms fail by 1890.

1865 May 8. Ft. Selden is established near Radium Springs to guard against Apaches. It closes in 1891.

1865 The flooding Rio Grande changes the course of the river, leaving Mesilla on its east bank, instead of its previous west bank of the river.

1867 March 2. Congress abolishes peonage in New Mexico.

1868 April 17. Juan Maria Augustini, the "Hermit," is murdered near La Cueva in the Organ Mountains and is buried in San Albino cemetery in Mesilla.

1869 First transcontinental railroad spans the United States.

1870 Las Cruces population reaches approx. 1,240.

1870 Sisters of Loretto purchase 15 acres to establish Loretto Academy. School closes June 30, 1944 and is sold to the Franciscan Fathers.

1871 Aug. 27. Republicans and Democrats, some of whom were drunk on campaign whiskey, riot in the Mesilla Plaza. Nine are killed and many are injured.

1873 The Mescalero Indian Reservation is established.

1875 March. St. James Episcopal Church is founded, the first Protestant church in the valley.

1877 Desert Lands Act offers 640 acres to homesteaders for 25 cents an acre down and the promise to irrigate the land within three years. Then for an additional $1 an acre, land was deeded to claimant. Often, however, water was not available. The act is regarded as a failure.

1876 Military telegraph line links Santa Fe, Las Cruces and Mesilla to the Arizona-San Diego military line.

1880 April 5. (Ceremony, April 25). The Atchison, Topeka and Santa Fe Railroad reaches Albuquerque.

1880 Gov. Lew Wallace publishes *Ben Hur.*

1881 April 13. At the Mesilla courthouse, Associate Judge William Bristol sentences Billy the Kid to death for killing Sheriff William Brady.

1881 April 26. (Work train, April 6). The AT&SF Railroad reaches Las Cruces.

1881 May 13. (Ceremony, May 26) Southern Pacific Railroad reaches El Paso. June (date not certain), AT&SF reaches El Paso.

1881 July 14. Pat Garrett kills Billy the Kid at Fort Sumner.

1882 Jan. County seat is moved from Mesilla to Las Cruces.

1883 May. U.S. Land Office moves to Las Cruces from Mesilla.

1883 June. Third Judicial District Court moves to Las Cruces from Mesilla.

1883 First Presbyterian Church is organized in Las Cruces.

1884 A group of Faithists establish Shalam Colony on the banks of the Rio Grande. The utopian colony for orphans and foundlings closes in 1907.

1888 Sept. 17. Las Cruces College opens with 64 pupils. Tuition is $40 a year.

1888 Sept. El Paso del Norte is renamed Juárez.

1890 Las Cruces population is 2,340; Mesilla, 1,389.

1890 Las Cruces College becomes New Mexico College of Agriculture and Mechanic Arts.

1890s Severe drought reduces ranching industry that relies on the towns of the Mesilla Valley as primary supply points.

1892 Oct. Women's Literary Club is founded.

1893 March 9. Samuel Steel, the college's only senior, is murdered during a hold-up by a drunken cowboy.

1893 South Ward School opens as first public school in Las Cruces on the corner of Alameda and Amador in an existing two-room adobe building. Building built about 1882, at one time housed the Las Cruces College. School closes in 1926, razed in 1935. New building built in 1935, destroyed by fire in 1956. School administration office built on site, vacated in 1991, destroyed by fire May 1991.

1894 Jan. 1. The University of New Mexico defeats the Aggies 18-6 in the first intercollegiate football game in New Mexico.

1894 Women's Improvement Association is founded.

1896 Feb. 1. Col. Albert Fountain and his nine-year-old son Henry are last seen near Chalk Hill in the Tularosa Basin. Oliver Lee is tried and acquited. The mystery remains unsolved.

1896 Lucero School opens in an old adobe church building on Church St. near Picacho St.

1898 The Spanish-American War begins. Theodore Roosevelt recruits Rough Riders in the Las Cruces area. War ends in 10 weeks.

1899 First Baptist Church is established.

1900 Las Cruces population is 2,906; Mesilla 1,274.

1900 Nationwide weekly pay averages $10; man's shirt costs 50 cents.

1901 Hemlines creep up to women's ankles and higher as women begin driving.

1902 June. U.S. Reclamation Act commits the government to providing water for reclaiming semi-arid and arid public lands in 16 western states including New Mexico.

1904 April 30. World's Fair opens in St. Louis.

1904 Central School is built and consists of eight rooms in a two-story brick building at the corner of Las Cruces Ave. and Alameda.

1904 Work begins on Panama Canal. Opens in 1914.

1905 May 3. First National Bank of Las Cruces is founded.

1906 May 21. The U.S. and Mexico enter into a treaty in which the U.S. agrees to furnish 60,000 acre-feet of water a year from the Rio Grande to Mexico.

1907 Las Cruces is officially incorporated as a town.

1908 Feb. 29. Pat Garrett is shot and killed on his way to Las Cruces from his ranch near Organ.

1910 Las Cruces population reaches 3,836; Mesilla, 1,025.

1911 March. Theodore Roosevelt makes a brief stop at the Las Cruces train depot.

1911 Construction begins on Elephant Butte Dam.

1912 Jan. 6. The territory of New Mexico becomes a state.

1916 March 9. Pancho Villa raids Columbus, New Mexico, killing 17.

1916 May 13. Elephant Butte Dam is completed at a cost of $7.2 million.

1917 April 6. U.S. enters World War I. June 17. First draft, men 21-30.

1917 Fall. "O Fair New Mexico," written by the daughter of Sheriff Pat Garrett, becomes the state song.

1918 Nov. 11. World War I ends when Germany and Allies sign armistice. Veterans come seeking land. Wounded veterans do not have to pay taxes.

1918 Worldwide flu epidemic strikes; by 1920, 22 million are dead.

1919 Jan. 16. Prohibition against the sale of liquor becomes law.

1920 Las Cruces population is 3,969; Mesilla, 1,011.

1920 Ralph W. Goddard founds KOB radio station, the first in the state.

1921 Albert B. Fall is appointed Secretary of the Interior.

1922 Geologists discover oil in New Mexico.

1922 Congress confirms Indian title to Mescalero Indian Reservation.

1923 Dec. The Las Cruces Board of Trustees requires fortune tellers and palm readers to be licensed.

1924 Branigan Library is built at a cost of $6,000.

1925 Union High School District is formed; Union High School is built.

1926 Las Cruces schools are segregated on the first day of the school term when Black students are moved to the Phillip's Chapel, property of the African Church. The schools are integrated in 1954.

1926 Deane Stahmann and his father buy 2,900 acres of the Santo Tomas farm; in 1936 Deane Stahmann buys the 1,100-acre Snow Farm.

1927 Sept. 4. Holy Cross School opens.

1927 May. The keeping of peacocks in Las Cruces becomes a misdemeanor.

1928 May. The Las Cruces Board of Trustees passes an ordinance providing for street light installation.

1929 Oct. 24. The stock market crashes bringing on the Depression.

1930 Las Cruces population is 5,811; Mesilla, 1,600.

1933 Clyde Tombaugh, while working in Arizona, discovers the planet Pluto.

1934 June. The Las Cruces Board of Trustees regulates the flying of airplanes to an altitude of no less than 1,000 feet and prohibits stunt flying.

1937 Doc Noss reportedly discovers gold and religious articles inside Victoria Peak.

1939 Sept. 1. Germany invades Poland. Sept 3. France and England declare war against Germany. World War II begins.

1939 The lobo, or gray wolf, is nearly extinct; only 30 remain in New Mexico.

1940 Las Cruces population is 8,385; Mesilla, no count; El Paso, 100,000; Albuquerque, 35,000.

1941 Dec. 7. Japan bombs Pearl Harbor. Dec. 8. U.S. and England declare war against Japan. Ft. Bliss has 25,000 soldiers.

1941 Court Junior High is built on Court St. with WPA labor.

1942 June. Manhatten Project is formed.

1944 Sept. 7. U.S. Goverment selects the Jornada del Muerto as the Trinity Site.

1945 July 9. White Sands Proving Ground is established.

1945 July 16, 5:29:45 a.m. The first atomic bomb is exploded at the Trinity Site in the Tularosa Basin.

1945 U.S. drops atomic bombs on Japan. World War II ends.

1946 Las Cruces is incorporated as a city.

1947 White Sands School opens in a one-room barracks with 14 elementary school students.

1948 Feb. 15. City bus line opens. Fare 10 cents. Shuts down a few months later.

1949 April 16. The body of Cricket Coogler is found. The unsolved case eventually involves officials in local and state government.

1949 Oct. 9-15. Las Cruces celebrates its centennial.

1950 The population of Las Cruces is 12,325; Mesilla, 1,264; El Paso, 130,345.

1956 Las Cruces High School opens for classes in its new building on El Paseo and Boutz.

1957 Oct. 1. The Soviet Union launches Sputnik.

1958 White Sands Proving Ground changes its name to White Sands Missile Range.

1958 Dec. 17. New Mexico College of Agriculture and Mechanic Arts becomes New Mexico State University. Name change legalized in 1960.

1960 Las Cruces loses some of its rural character as population increases to 29,367; Mesilla, 1,264.

1962 June. First National Bank opens on Loretto property.

1963 Las Cruces Community Theater created.

1965 March. Loretto Mall opens.

1965 Mayfield High School opens on Valley Dr.

1966-68 Passenger service to Las Cruces on Atcheson, Topeka and Santa Fe Railroad is phased out.

1967 Ten-story First National Bank Tower opens.

1967 Oct. 18. St. Genevieve's Catholic Church is razed. Bank buys property.

1970 Las Cruces, at 37,857, becomes the largest city in southern New Mexico.

1971 Sept. Elephant Butte Irrigation District pays off debt to the Bureau of Reclamation.

1973 Jan. 27. Viet Nam War ends.

1973 Feb. 21-23. Students participate in Intervisitation Riot at NMSU.

1976 Albert Johnson becomes the first black mayor of Las Cruces.

1978 Sept. 16. Capacity crowd watches the New Mexico State University football team defeat the University of Texas at El Paso in its new 30,343-seat stadium 35-32.

1979-80 Season. Mark Medoff receives Tony Award for "Children of a Lesser God." Play was first performed at NMSU.

1980 Las Cruces is designated as an urban area with 44,902 people; Mesilla totals 2,019.

1981 Summer. Mesilla Valley Mall opens.

1981 About 1,000 Indians of predominantly Mescalero lineage live on the Mescalero Reservation.

1980 Sept. 5. El Paso files lawsuit for right to drill ground water in New Mexico.

1982 The Space Shuttle lands at White Sands.

1988 July. Atcheson, Topeka and Santa Fe Railway closes freight operations at Las Cruces depot.

1990 Las Cruces population reaches 62,126 with 135,510 in the county; Mesilla drops to 1,975; El Paso reaches 504,000.

1991 May 20. Jarvis Garrett (Pat Garrett's youngest and last surviving child) dies in Albuquerque.

1991 May 7. El Paso drops water suit against New Mexico.

1993 Aug. 19. Oñate High School opens in its new building on Northeast Main St.

INDEX

*Page numbers noted with * refer to photograph captions.*

THANKS

Cheryl Wilson • Linda Blazer • Patricia McCann • Tim Blevins • New Mexico State University Library • Don Dresp • Marjorie Day • Mark Pendleton • Patricia Greathouse • Branigan Memorial Library • Leslie Blair • New Mexico Water Resources Research Institute Library • Gerald W. Thomas • Darlis Miller • Jeffrey P. Brown • Ira G. Clark • Jim Williams • Anthony Popp • Robert Smiggen • Pam Pacanowski • Pat Miles • New Mexico State University • David T. Kirkpatrick • Human Systems Research, Inc. • Patrick Beckett • COAS Research • Robert G. Myers • U.S. Geological Survey • Jim Eckles • White Sands Public Information Office • Jo Galvan • Las Cruces Public Schools • John Keith • Vincent Benegas • City of Las Cruces • Gordon Tilney • Greater Las Cruces Economic Development Council • Teresa Hanley • Bill Diven • Nancy Tod • John P. Wilson • Mary D. Taylor • Opal Lee Priestley • Lee Gemoets • Alice Gruver • Nancy Peters Hastings • Cheryl Thornburg • Rem Alley • Leon Metz • John Grassham • Paxton Price • Ilsa Altshool • Dona Ana County Historical Society • Nancy Jenkins • Frank Jenkins • Dona Ana County Archeological Society • Toni Martinez • Darlene Reeves • Jim Harris